THE BROWN RICE COOKBOOK

Brown rice is more than just nutritious — it is delicious, with a flavour white rice cannot match. Here is information, advice and a wide range of varied recipes to help you make full use of this wholesome healthfood.

D0011938

Also by Craig Sams
ABOUT MACROBIOTICS

Other books in this series
BAKING BETTER BREADS
CAKES, SCONES AND BISCUITS
INDIAN CURRIES
ITALIAN DISHES
MAGIC OF TOFU
ORIENTAL DISHES
PASTA DISHES
PIES, BAKES AND CASSEROLES
PIZZAS AND PANCAKES
QUICHES AND FLANS
SALADS
SIMPLE AND SPEEDY WHOLEFOOD COOKING
VEGETARIAN DINNER PARTIES
WHOLEFOOD LUNCH BOX

THE BROWN RICE COOKBOOK
A Selection of Delicious Wholesome Recipes

by

CRAIG and ANN SAMS

Illustrated by Clive Birch

THORSONS PUBLISHERS LIMITED
Wellingborough, Northamptonshire

First published 1980
Second edition (revised, enlarged
and reset, June 1983)
Second Impression September 1983

British Library Cataloguing in Publication Data

Sams, Craig
  The brown rice cookbook. 2nd rev. ed.
  1. Cookery (Rice)   2. Rice, Unpolished
  I. Title   II. Sams, Ann
  641.6'318   TX809.R5

ISBN 0-7225-0823-9

Printed in Great Britain by
Richard Clay (The Chaucer Press) Ltd,
Bungay, Suffolk

CONTENTS

A British standard measuring cupful
contains 10 fl oz (275ml)

An American standard measuring cupful
contains 8 fl oz (225ml)

INTRODUCTION

Recent years have seen a great increase in the consumption and availability of brown rice. Whereas white rice was once the only variety known, brown rice now enjoys widespread popularity not only among dedicated healthfood users but also with many cooks who use it as a flavoursome ingredient in their culinary repertoire.

In the early 1960's many people in Europe and the U.S.A. were attracted to the ideas of Georges Ohsawa, a Japanese who had rediscovered the importance of dietary balance in traditional Eastern medicine. Guided by the principle that digestive health underpins the total condition of the body he taught macrobiotics, a dietary system in which brown rice plays a major role. With the general awakening of interest in Eastern ideas and with the increase in awareness of bodily health, brown rice and associated foods became more widely used. In the world of pop music the expression 'brown rice sandwiches' was used in association with the musicians who adopted wholefood diets. Then in the mid-1970's came the bran boom with an upsurge in demand for wholewheat bread, brown rice, pop corn and beans. In fact anything with that magic ingredient — 'dietary fibre' — was hailed by orthodox medicine as the cure for all kinds of bodily ills. The decline in consumption of white bread is now paralleled by a decrease in white sugar consumption, the first in peacetime in a century, as a new awareness of the importance of diet to health develops.

Brown rice is more than just nutritious — it is delicious, with a full, nutty flavour that white rice can never match. It is versatile, enhancing a wide variety of other foods in infinite combinations. Why, then, did brown rice ever lose its once pre-eminent position to white rice? The answer lies partly in the fact that while white rice will keep almost indefinitely, brown rice should be fresh. It attracts insects once it has been husked, so it needs more care in storage and more attention to efficient distribution.

In the nineteenth and early twentieth centuries it was economically convenient to have rice in a form that was easily stored, quickly cooked, and long-lasting. Even today the extra attention that handling brown rice requires means that it sells at a higher price, even though it has not been processed as much as white rice. Also, brown rice of poor quality is visibly less attractive. Polishing conceals a multitude of faults. Powdered talc and glucose are also frequently dusted over white rice to enhance its appearance, so if you do use white rice it is a good idea to wash it thoroughly before preparation.

Most of the recipes in this book will work with different varieties of rice, or with mixtures of more than one kind.

1.

VARIETIES OF RICE

Rice is believed to have originally been grown from wild plants that thrived in Indonesia and South-East Asia. Now it is to be found on every continent, growing in a wide variety of climates and conditions. The numerous varieties of rice that exist are an indication of both regional taste and geographical differences. The main mode of classification of rice is by the size of the grain: short, medium, or long.

Short Grain

Short grain rice grains are about 5mm in length and have a soft texture when cooked. Commonly used in puddings, short grain rice has a wide variety of savoury uses and is particularly good when served with sauces or with vegetables. It can be served with an ice-cream scoop. A slightly glutinous strain of short grain rice is cultivated in Japan and is being grown increasingly in Italy, France, Spain, and California in response to demand for this variety from brown rice eaters.

Medium Grain

Medium grain rice is similar to short grain but longer, about 6mm. Grown in Italy and the U.S.A., its appeal is mainly in the form of white rice, although in its brown form it is absorbent and used in dishes with yogurt or vegetable sauces.

Long Grain

Long grain rice is slender in shape and can be from 6-8mm in length. The grains are dry when cooked and do not stick to each other. The best varieties of long grain rice are grown in sub-tropical climates, particularly Texas, Surinam, and Thailand.

Similar to long grain rice in thinness but shorter and somewhat chewier in texture are Basmati rice and California long grain rice.

Sweet Brown Rice
Sweet brown rice is a very glutinous variety originating from Japan. Its sweet flavour and moist texture when cooked make it ideal for desserts where one wishes to keep sweeteners to a minimum, and also as an addition to some other variety of rice being cooked.

Red Rice
This grows in South-East Asia and is similar to long grain in shape. Because it is hardy it is grown where other rice crops would not thrive. It is dull in colour when polished so generally the whole grains are eaten by poorer people or used as animal feed. A purplish-black long grain variety is grown in China and can sometimes be found in Chinese grocers. Green grains may appear in some varieties of brown rice, particularly from France and Italy. These are fully-ripened grains which have not had sufficient sunshine during their final ripening to turn a golden-brown colour. Once cooked, these grains are similar to the browner grains in every respect.

White Rice
Almost any of the above varieties of rice can be turned into white rice by the removal of the bran layers of the grain and the germ to leave the starchy white kernel. The bran and germ contain almost all the vitamins and minerals and oils of the grain, as well as much of the protein.

The main disadvantages of using white rice, apart from the loss of nutritive elements comes from the loss of the high-fibre bran layers of the grain. The effect of consuming bran is twofold: firstly, the appetitie is satisfied at a reasonable level — a feeling of fullness arises due to the very bulk of the bran and overeating leading to obesity is less likely to occur. Secondly, the fibre element helps speed and facilitate the digestive process thereby reducing the likelihood of diseases of the intestine.

Parboiled Rice

Sometimes called 'brown' rice, this is a processed rice that is the result of an attempt to avoid the worst effects of rice-milling. The whole unhusked grains of rice are immersed in hot water and some of the B-vitamins and soluble minerals in the bran and germ soak into the starchy kernel. The grains are then dried and the bran and germ are removed. The result is a rice that has a dull brown colour, a little flavour, and just enough vitamins to keep the consumer from developing beri-beri or pellagra, two diseases that arise directly from the refining of rice where it is a staple part of the diet.

Wild Rice

Wild rice is not really a member of the family of the other rices but is an aquatic grass whose large dark grains stand on long stalks in the lakes of Canada and North Central United States. The grains are harvested by threshing the heads of the plants against the inside hull of a canoe. Wild rice is expensive, but a little mixed with long grain rice before cooking can have a considerable effect.

About Organic Rice

For extra enjoyment of the recipes in this book, we recommend that you use organically grown rice whenever possible. With some foods the conditions under which they are grown is not of overriding importance, but with brown rice the flavour and quality differences are considerable. The leading producers of organically grown rice are in California and in Northern Italy. In both cases, their output is widely regarded as being noticeably superior in taste and quality. (The California growers even supply rice to breeders of ornamental swans: the breeders have found that only with organic rice can they be sure that the swans breed true from generation to generation.)

In Italy, a large area of the upper reaches of the River Po has come under organic cultivation by a group of farmers who realized that modern methods threatened to undermine the heritage of the rice paddies that their families had worked for centuries. In rice farming the decision to grow organically must be a collective one as the water is shared by all, and if one farmer uses chemicals, every farmer further down the irrigation network does as well. In order to ensure a pure water supply to begin with, the farmers have their water piped from a spring that is fed by melted Alpine snow. For natural fertility in the soil they use farmyard and vegetable composts instead of chemical fertilizers. In this way the rice grows strong and healthy, and is more immune to insects and diseases. Every third year the land is sown with a cover crop such as alfalfa to restore fertility.

We always use organically grown rice, although the price can be up to 25 per cent higher than ordinary rice. This works out to only pennies per serving, a small price to pay for a big gain in the quality of a food that is the heart of a meal.

2.

CHOOSING YOUR INGREDIENTS

Rice and Beans

Brown rice is rich in a wide variety of essential amino acids, the constituent proteins needed for tissue development and growth. Combined with the members of the bean family, which contain other amino acids, one obtains a range of amino acids that exceeds the constituents of either of the foods taken separately. This effect, known as synergy, applies to other combinations of cereals and pulses, such as bread and lentil soup.

To get the full benefit of this synergistic effect, the rice and beans should be eaten at the same meal. In general, however, they cannot be cooked together, although there are some exceptions, e.g. pre-soaked adzuki beans can be cooked with rice together in a pressure cooker — the cooking periods are the same for both.

Soaking beans for at least twelve hours is a very important aspect of the preparation process: not only are the beans easier to cook to a soft consistency, but in the soaking period the dormant life force of the bean is activated, and it begins the changes that will in a few days lead to sprouting and the development of roots, stalk and leaves.

This little change makes a great difference to the digestibility and the nutrient availability of the cooked bean — it is no good eating a food because a laboratory analysis shows that it is rich in protein if it gives you indigestion, flatulence and your digestive system only extracts a small part of the available nutritional content.

Pythagoras would not let his students eat beans because he believed they inhibited the higher intellectual processes. However, it is likely that this was because the prevalent bean of classical Greece was the fava bean — harmless in itself but with a hard brown skin which, if regularly eaten, can lead to favism, symptoms of which are deterioration of vision and mental faculties. Foods such as adzuki beans, chick peas, lentils, and black soyabeans in particular, when properly cooked, can only enhance the functioning of mind and body.

Vegetables

As with grains and beans, vegetables are that much better when organically grown. The advantages of eating foods that do not contain either external residues of insecticides or internal traces of systemic herbicides need little elaboration. Agricultural chemicals are particularly damaging to the body's cleansing organs like the kidneys and liver, and they accumulate in the body's fat reserves, storing future harm. It takes several generations for the human body to adapt to environmental changes, small consolation if you are exposing yourself to them now.

Soya Sauce

Soya sauce is a name that covers a multitude of brown seasonings. At one end of the spectrum is the manufactured soya sauce containing hydrolyzed vegetable proteins, caramel colouring, monosodium glutamate, salt, and water. Real soya sauce or *shoyu* is a naturally fermented product made from a broth of soyabeans and wheat, carefully matured for over a year. *Tamari* soya sauce is also fermented, from soyabeans alone, and has a rich savoury flavour. The glutamic acid that derives from the soyabeans used is not only a flavour enhancer but also a valuable amino acid, or basic protein.

Miso soyabean *purée* is made from soyabeans and various cereals and is a paste similar in flavour to soya sauce. It is also naturally fermented over a long period. From Japan, the most popular variety is *genmai miso* which is made from brown rice and soyabeans and has a savoury/sweet flavour with none of the bitterness of some *misos*.

Oil

As with white rice, popular taste in a food to some extent reflects the most convenient form from the food manufacturer's or processor's point of view. Refined oils have no flavour of their own, and store well with the addition of a small amount of antioxidant chemicals. Unrefined oils have distinctive flavours, of which olive oil is best known, and have a higher level of free fatty acids which can lead eventually to rancidity in old or badly stored oils. Fresh unrefined oils extracted without solvent chemicals make an incomparable difference to dishes in which they are used.

Seaweeds and Wild Vegetables
These can, when used in small quantities, provide trace elements that the body needs and which are lacking in foods grown in regularly cultivated ground. *Kombu, wakame*, and *arame* from Japan, as well as dulse from Ireland, provide piquant tastes that harmonize with most foods. Wild vegetables such as nettles and fat-hen can be used with, or in place of, spinach where greens are called for. Chickweed is good in salads, and young burdock roots are quite a good substitute for other root vegetables.

Sugar
Sugar is not included in any of the recipes that follow. Dried fruits, concentrated fruit juices, or malt extract all provide sweetness that does not have the same unbalancing effect on the blood-sugar levels as cane or beet sugars and glucose. The over-consumption of refined sugars not only leads to obesity and disease but also undermines one's sense of taste and ability to enjoy the less pronounced sweetness that is present in other foods.

Salt
Sea salt is preferred because, being unrefined, it contains not only sodium chloride but many valuable trace minerals as well. Natural crystal salt, mined in Cheshire, can be obtained unrefined in health food shops and many supermarkets and derives from a sea that dried up in prehistoric times — it has all the qualities of sea salt.

Dried Fruit
Whenever possible dried fruit that has not been treated with sulphur

dioxide should be used as it has more flavour and sweetness. Raisins and sultanas are frequently treated with liquid paraffin. This assists cake manufacturers and fruit packers as the fruit flows freely and does not stick together, but is hardly necessary for domestic use.

Kitchen Utensils

All kitchen utensils should be made of non-reactive materials like stainless steel or glass. Aluminium can give off flavours and colours, enamel pans chip, and cast-iron is best used for frying rather than boiling. The extra cost in obtaining stainless steel serving spoons is repaid by their longer usable life. Many plated utensils soon lose their outer finish and this goes straight into your food.

Note: Unless otherwise stated, all recipes serve six.

3.

COOKING BROWN RICE

Most of the recipes in this book call for pre-cooked rice. There are a variety of methods for preparing the uncooked grains, and you may find that you will want to vary the cooking times, salt levels, or proportion of water used to suit your personal taste.

BOILED BROWN RICE

Always check your rice for the presence of any foreign bodies; a small stone or other particle can spoil someone's enjoyment of an entire meal. There is no pre-cleaning method that is 100 per cent effective, so the extra precaution of picking over your rice is worth the minute or two it may take.

Then wash your rice. You can simply place the saucepan under a running tap and let the water flow over the top, or shake it in water in a closed container and then pour away the water through a strainer, either way you get rid of dust and dirt that may detract from the flavour of the rice.

Imperial (Metric)
2 cupsful water
1 cupful brown rice
½ teaspoonful sea salt

American
2½ cupsful water
1¼ cupsful brown rice
½ teaspoonful sea salt

1. Bring the water, rice and salt to the boil and allow to boil for 3 minutes.

2. Reduce heat to lowest possible level and simmer, covered, for 40 minutes to one hour or until water has all been absorbed and rice is just beginning to scorch.

3. Remove from heat, stir, let stand for 5 minutes, and it is ready to serve. Do not stir rice while it is cooking.

PRESSURE-COOKED BROWN RICE

Because there is less evaporation you can use less water when pressure-cooking rice. For larger quantities you can reduce the proportion of water used from that given below.

Imperial (Metric)
1 cupful brown rice
1½ cupsful water
¼-½ teaspoonful sea salt

American
1¼ cupsful brown rice
1⅔ cupsful water
¼-½ teaspoonful sea salt

1. Bring combined ingredients to full pressure, then lower heat and cook for 35-45 minutes.

2. Remove from heat and let stand for at least ten minutes.

3. Remove cover, mix rice, and serve.

BAKED BROWN RICE

Imperial (Metric)	American
2 cupsful brown rice	2½ cupsful brown rice
3-3½ cupsful water	3¾-4⅓ cupsful water
½ teaspoonful sea salt	½ teaspoonful sea salt

1. For an extra nutty flavour stir the rice in a dry frying pan on top of the cooker until it is warm and becomes a golden brown.

2. Place in a covered casserole with the water and salt and bake for 45 minutes in a 350°F/180°C (Gas Mark 4) oven.

3. Remove and allow to cool a bit before serving as it is much hotter straight from the pan than boiled rice.

STEAMED BROWN RICE

Left-over cooked brown rice can be steamed to reheat it before use. It is also possible to obtain tender fluffy rice using the following method. This is particularly recommended for long grain rice.

Imperial (Metric)	American
1½ cupsful brown rice	1⅔ cupsful brown rice
4 cupsful water	5 cupsful water
1½ teaspoonsful sea salt	1½ teaspoonsful sea salt

1. Sprinkle the rice into the boiling water and add the salt.

2. When all the rice is added stir for a moment and boil for 10-15 minutes. The grains should be tender but still brittle in the middle.

3. Rinse the grains in hot water and then wrap in a tea towel or cheesecloth and steam in a colander or steamer for about 30 minutes.

Variations

Add *tamari* or *shoyu* soyasauce to the rice instead of sea salt. A few *sautéd* vegetables such as onions or celery can be added to the rice when cooking. Dried chestnuts, with two parts of water extra added, impart their sweet flavour to cooking rice. Alternatively, add a small proportion of uncooked barley, rye, or wheat to the rice. For extra tenderness, pre-soak these grains before adding.

If you have a temperature control that will enable you to bake at a low temperature, baked rice can be made overnight, using the same recipe as above but cooking at a lower temperature. The scorched and yellowish rice at the bottom of the pan can be removed by sprinkling it with water and reheating the pan for a few minutes. This rice is very tasty and chewy, and delicious dipped in a mixture of soya sauce, ginger and chopped green onions.

SAFFRON RICE

Imperial (Metric)
2 cupsful long grain brown rice
3 cupsful water
1 teaspoonful turmeric or
  2 strands saffron*

American
2½ cupsful long grain brown rice
3¾ cupsful water
1 teaspoonful turmeric or
  2 strands saffron*

Bring the rice and water to the boil, add the saffron or turmeric and simmer gently in a covered pan for 40 minutes.

*Naturally saffron is preferable but it is always very expensive and sometimes hard to find, in which case turmeric is a good substitute.

RICE CREAM CEREAL

Purée cooked brown rice with extra water and cook to a soft mushy consistency. The resulting cereal can be seasoned to taste for a breakfast cereal, and for invalids or infants.

POPPED RICE

Popped brown rice is not a light fluffy product like pop corn, but it is deliciously crunchy and the pre-soaking period enhances the sweetness of the grains. Once you have popped your rice it can be stored for several weeks in an airtight jar or even a thick polythene bag, tightly sealed and kept in the fridge, to be used as required.

Try oven-toasting pumpkin seeds, sesame seeds or sunflower seeds, then lightly sprinkle them with natural soya sauce, and mix with popped rice. You will have a delicious snack that is irrestible to children and adults alike and, because of the chewing it requires, provides excellent exercise for the teeth and gums.

To pop brown rice:
Soak 2/2½ (US) cupsful of rice in water — enough to cover well. Leave overnight then change water daily for three more days. Finally rinse well and empty rice to about half-inch depth into a heavy-bottomed frying-pan/skillet over medium heat, stirring constantly until rice is popped and brown. Remove from frying-pan/skillet and season with soya sauce while still hot.

IN PLACE OF WATER

Brown rice can be prepared with other liquids besides water. The flavours or colours obtained in this way can subtly enhance the dish in which the rice is used. One caution, however — if you are using a liquid that has a high level of dissolved solids such as tomato or mushroom soup the risk of scorching is greatly increased.

The following liquids are good with rice:

Tea — Japanese green tea or twig tea both harmonize well with the flavour of rice. You can also make various herbal teas that have a distinctive flavour. Try anise, dillseed, tarragon, or lovage (for a celery-like flavour).

Stock — Boil a strip of *kombu* seaweed in water with a sliced onion, a dash of *shoyu* (real soya sauce), a bay leaf, a few cloves of garlic and a dried red pepper. Strain before boiling with the rice.

For rice puddings or when rice is being used in a curry or other spice dish, then a few cloves, cinnamon quills or mace, soaked in boiling water for a few hours, will lend a spicy bouquet to rice.

For colour, chop and boil a beetroot in the water you are using for your rice and the rice will come out a pinkish colour. Saffron or turmeric will give a yellow colour.

4.

SOUPS

RICE SOUP

Imperial (Metric)	American
1 cupful chopped onions	1¼ cupsful chopped onions
1 cupful brown rice	1¼ cupsful brown rice
Pinch each of thyme, marjoram and sea salt	Pinch each of thyme, marjoram and sea salt
1 bay leaf	1 bay leaf
4 pints (2 litres) boiling water	4½ pints boiling water
1 tablespoonful *tamari*	1 tablespoonful *tamari*
1 cupful chick peas or haricot beans, pre-cooked	1¼ cupsful garbanzo beans or dried beans, pre-cooked

1. *Sauté* first six ingredients until onions are transparent.

2. Add boiling water and pressure cook for 30 minutes. Push through strainer.

3. Add *tamari* and chick peas (garbanzo beans) or haricot (dried) beans.

RICE, VEGETABLE AND TOFU SOUP

Imperial (Metric)	American
1 stalk celery, diced	1 stalk celery, diced
1 carrot, diced	1 carrot, diced
4 mushrooms, thinly sliced	4 mushrooms, thinly sliced
1½ tablespoonful vegetable oil	1½ tablespoonful vegetable oil
3 cupsful vegetable stock	3¾ cupsful vegetable stock
1 cupful brown rice	1¼ cupsful brown rice
1 teaspoonful grated ginger	1 teaspoonful grated ginger
1½ tablespoonsful real soya sauce	1½ tablespoonsful real soya sauce
¼ teaspoonful sea salt	¼ teaspoonful sea salt
2 teaspoonsful *kuzu*, dissolved in a little water	2 teaspoonsful *kuzu*, dissolved in a little water
6 oz (150g) tofu, cut into small cubes	1 cupful tofu, cut into small cubes

1. *Sauté* the celery, carrots and mushrooms in the oil for 5 minutes or until tender. Set aside.

2. Mix the stock, rice, ginger and soya sauce together. Bring to the boil and stir in the *kuzu*.

3. When thickened, stir in the vegetables and the tofu. Bring back to the boil and serve immediately.

BLENDED RICE AND ONION SOUP

Imperial (Metric)
1 large onion, finely chopped
1 tablespoonful vegetable oil
2 cupsful cooked brown rice
2 tablespoonsful oatflakes
1 pint (½ litre) water
1 tablespoonful real soya sauce
Parsley, finely chopped

American
1 large onion, finely chopped
1 tablespoonful vegetable oil
2½ cupsful cooked brown rice
2 tablespoonsful oatflakes
2½ cupsful water
1 tablespoonful real soya sauce
Parsley, finely chopped

1. *Sauté* the onion in the oil until transparent.

2. Add the rice, oatflakes and water and bring to the boil. Simmer for 20 minutes.

3. Stir in the soya sauce then blend in a liquidizer. Serve sprinkled with chopped parsley.

LEMON SOUP

Imperial (Metric)	American
2½ pints (1¼ litres) vegetable stock	6⅓ cupsful vegetable stock
1 cupful cooked long grain brown rice	1¼ cupsful cooked long grain brown rice
1 lemon	1 lemon
3 eggs	3 eggs
Real soya sauce	Real soya sauce

1. Heat the stock to boiling and add cooked rice. Remove from heat.

2. Squeeze the lemon and beat the juice with the eggs, diluting this mixture with a little of the stock.

3. When the mixture is smooth, combine with the stock and cook gently for 2 to 3 minutes. Do *not* bring to the boil.

4. Season with soya sauce and serve.

NETTLE SOUP WITH BROWN RICE
(Pick the nettles for this recipe before June.)

Imperial (Metric)
2 lb (1 kilo) nettles
1 onion, finely chopped
2 cloves garlic, finely chopped
1 tablespoonful vegetable oil
3 pints (1½ litres) water or
  vegetable stock
1 cupful cooked brown rice
1 teaspoonful sea salt
1 teaspoonful freshly ground black
  pepper

American
2 pounds nettles
1 onion, finely chopped
2 cloves garlic, finely chopped
1 tablespoonful vegetable oil
7½ cupful water or vegetable
  stock
1¼ cupful cooked brown rice
1 teaspoonful sea salt
1 teaspoonful freshly ground black
  pepper

1. Wearing gloves, remove the tops and tender young leaves of the nettles and discard the stalks.

2. *Sauté* the onion and garlic in the oil for a few minutes.

3. Add the nettles and cook for another few minutes.

4. Add the stock and bring to the boil, then stir in the rice and seasonings.

5. Simmer gently for at least 45 minutes, then adjust seasoning and add more water as required.

MISO SOUP WITH BROWN RICE

No Japanese would dream of venturing forth in the morning without a fortifying bowl of *miso* soup. There are as many ways to prepare *miso* soup as there are leftover vegetables and grains — all have their value extended and their flavour enhanced by being cooked in a broth with *miso*. The 18-month fermentation period of a good quality *miso* enables the enzymes that act on the soya beans and grains to draw out the deepest and subtlest components of flavour and it is hard to believe that this flavoursome food can be the transformation of such bland ingredients. That's the wonder of enzymes!

Miso soup can be anything from a thin broth to a rich conglomeration of ingredients. The following recipe uses the mellow-flavoured *genmai miso* which is made with brown rice and soya beans.

Imperial (Metric)	American
1 onion, chopped	1 onion, chopped
1 tablespoonful vegetable oil	1 tablespoonful vegetable oil
2 carrots, peeled and finely chopped	2 carrots, peeled and finely chopped
2 cloves garlic, finely chopped	2 cloves garlic, finely chopped
1 cupful bean sprouts	1¼ cupsful bean sprouts
2 cupsful cooked brown rice	2½ cupsful cooked brown rice
3 pints (1½ litres) water or vegetable stock	7½ cupsful water or vegetable stock
½ cupful *genmai miso*	½ cupful *genmai miso*
2 teaspoonsful kelp powder	2 teaspoonsful kelp powder
2 teaspoonsful lemon juice or cider vinegar	2 teaspoonsful lemon juice or cider vinegar
1 teaspoonful concentrated apple juice	1 teaspoonful concentrated apple juice
½ teaspoonful cayenne	½ teaspoonful cayenne

1. *Sauté* the onions until translucent, then add the remaining vegetables and *sauté* a further 5 minutes.

2. Add the rice and water or stock and boil for 10 minutes.

3. Combine the *miso* and remaining ingredients with one cupful of cold water and mix until smooth. Add to the soup and bring

just to the boil before serving. (Chopped parsley or watercress may be sprinkled on top.)

Variation:
The apple juice, lemon juice and cayenne are optional. *Kombu* or *wakame* seaweed can replace the kelp powder. For a change, a few spoonsful of *puréed* tomatoes enhance the flavour.

Note: Why do we recommend peeled carrots? Although organically grown vegetables are always preferable, they are not always obtainable. The insecticide lindane is prohibited in Europe for all agricultural use except carrot growing. It is the only chemical that can sink in to the soil and permeate the carrot's outer skin sufficiently to deter the carrot fly.

5.

RICE AND VEGETABLES

This classic dish serves as a nutritious vegetarian staple meal and, despite the limitations implied by its title, the permutations are infinite. In his reflections on childhood days, Mao Tse Tung, remarkably, failed to moralize on the advantages or disadvantages of this diet. He merely remarked that his father, an ambitious middle peasant, turned his livestock into cash at the local market, and restricted young Mao to a diet of coarse unpolished rice and vegetables, with fish on rare occasions. While the diet no doubt did him nothing but good, who knows what rebellious resentment of the profit motive developed in his mind as he watched the live produce of his father's farm being trotted off to grace other people's tables.

RICE AND CARROTS

This is a quick and easy-to-prepare dish. When I first developed an appetite for regular helpings of brown rice, this featured so regularly on my menu that I later abandoned it altogether, to rediscover it with pleasure nearly fifteen years later for inclusion here.

Grate 3 medium-sized washed carrots on a coarse grater. *Sauté* grated carrots in a frying pan/skillet in 2/2½ (US) tablespoonsful of vegetable oil until the oil begins to acquire an orange tinge, then add 3/3½ (US) tablespoonsful of sesame seeds and *sauté* further until carrots are soft through. Serve as a bed for, or on a bed of, freshly boiled or steamed left-over brown rice.

MUSHROOM FRIED RICE

Imperial (Metric)
1 chopped onion
Vegetable oil
1 cupful sliced mushrooms
2 cupsful cooked long grain
  brown rice
Real soya sauce

American
1 chopped onion
Vegetable oil
1¼ cupsful sliced mushrooms
2½ cupsful cooked long grain
  brown rice
Real soya sauce

1. *Sauté* onion for 5 minutes, add mushrooms and cook until mushrooms are tender and cooked through.

2. Add the cooked rice and stir and fry for another 2/3 minutes, adding soya sauce to taste. Serve garnished with chopped parsley.

FRIED RICE AND VEGETABLES

Imperial (Metric)	American
1 tablespoonful sesame oil	1 tablespoonful sesame oil
1 onion, chopped	1 onion, chopped
4 cloves garlic, crushed	4 cloves garlic, crushed
1 teaspoonful ground cumin	1 teaspoonful ground cumin
1 carrot, chopped	1 carrot, chopped
1 swede, chopped	1 rutabaga, chopped
1 cupful bean sprouts	1¼ cupsful bean sprouts
4 oz (100g) frozen peas	1 cupful frozen peas
2 cupsful pre-cooked brown rice	2½ cupsful pre-cooked brown rice
1 teaspoonful real soya sauce	1 teaspoonful real soya sauce

1. Using a heavy frying pan (skillet), heat the oil and *sauté* the onion and garlic.

2. Add the cumin, then the carrot and swede (rutabaga).

3. Finally add the bean sprouts and peas and cook over a high heat, stirring constantly.

4. Add the rice and soya sauce and heat for a further 5 minutes.

BANANAS AND RICE

Throughout Latin America and South-East Asia, bananas are frequently used with rice, not for desserts but as a main meal. The original bananas are known as plantains, and although green in colour, are highly nutritious. Most bananas nowadays are the sweet yellow variety which, although higher in natural sugar content and lower in other nutritive qualities, cause little harm except in some of the producing countries where the natives have unwittingly substituted them for the plantain as their principal food.

Imperial (Metric)	American
2 onions, chopped	2 onions, chopped
Vegetable oil	Vegetable oil
3 cupsful cooked long grain brown rice	3¾ cupsful cooked long grain brown rice
Real soya sauce	Real soya sauce
4 eggs	4 eggs
4 bananas	4 bananas

1. *Sauté* the onions in oil until soft.

2. Add the cooked brown rice and heat together, seasoning with soya sauce.

3. Fry the eggs in oil in another pan 'sunnyside up'.

4. Place the onion-rice mixture on individual plates, and form a pit in the middle. Fill the pit with one fried egg.

5. Slice the bananas lengthwise and fry in the oil in which the eggs have been fried. When they are slightly browned at the edges, remove and place the strips of banana on the rice around the pit containing the egg.

6. Garnish with parsley or strips of raw carrot and serve.

Note: This recipe serves four.

RICE AND GREEN HERBS

Imperial (Metric)	American
2 cupsful brown rice	2½ cupsful brown rice
1 cupful pre-cooked spinach	1¼ cupsful pre-cooked spinach
8 spring onions	8 scallions
2 heaped tablespoonsful chopped mixed rosemary, thyme, marjoram, tarragon, summer savory	2½ heaped tablespoonsful chopped mixed rosemary, thyme, marjoram, tarragon, summer savory
1 teaspoonful grated lemon rind	1 teaspoonful grated lemon rind
1 teaspoonful sea salt	1 teaspoonful sea salt
1 or 2 cloves garlic	1 or 2 cloves garlic
½ teaspoonful black peppercorns	½ teaspoonful black peppercorns
1 teaspoonful lemon juice	1 teaspoonful lemon juice
2 teaspoonsful sunflower seed oil	2 teaspoonsful sunflower seed oil

1. Cook the rice until done, then let it cool.

2. Chop the spinach with the spring onions (scallions), combine with herbs and lemon rind and mix into the rice.

3. Crush the salt, garlic and peppercorns together and mix with the rice.

4. Cover and leave for ten minutes for the flavours to blend. Before serving sprinkle with lemon juice and the oil.

Note: This recipe can vary enormously depending on the herbs you use. We sometimes add chopped rue for a strong, bitter, pungent quality, and it is also delicious with a predominating fresh basil flavour, perhaps lightly sprinkled with crumbs of Caerphilly cheese.

TARRAGON RICE

Imperial (Metric)	**American**
2 onions, chopped	2 onions, chopped
3 cloves garlic, chopped	3 cloves garlic, chopped
½ lb (¼ kilo) green peas	1⅓ cupsful green peas
3 teaspoonsful dried tarragon	3 teaspoonsful dried tarragon
3 cupsful cooked brown rice	3¾ cupsful cooked brown rice

1. *Sauté* the onions until translucent, then add the garlic, peas and tarragon.

2. When the garlic is cooked, add the rice and cover it all with a watery version of the Basic Onion Sauce (page 49).

3. Simmer gently for 5 minutes and serve garnished with quartered lemons and parsley.

HERBED WILD RICE AND BROWN RICE MIXED

Wild rice is very expensive and often hard to get. Even when I do have some I mix it half and half with a long grain brown rice. But should no wild rice be available at all, then all the following recipes may be used with long grain brown rice instead.

Imperial (Metric)	American
2 tablespoonsful vegetable oil	2½ tablespoonsful vegetable oil
2 tablespoonsful spring onions, finely chopped	2½ tablespoonsful scallions, finely chopped
2 cloves garlic, finely chopped	2 cloves garlic, finely chopped
4 oz (100g) wild rice	½ cupful wild rice
4 oz (100g) long grain brown rice	½ cupful long grain brown rice
2 bay leaves	2 bay leaves
1 teaspoonful fresh thyme	1 teaspoonful fresh thyme
1 teaspoonful fresh basil	1 teaspoonful fresh basil
1 teaspoonful fresh marjoram	1 teaspoonful fresh marjoram
1½ cupsful water or vegetable stock	1⅔ cupsful water or vegetable stock
1 teaspoonful sea salt	1 teaspoonful sea salt
1 teaspoonful freshly ground black pepper	1 teaspoonful freshly ground black pepper

1. Heat the oil in a heavy-bottomed saucepan and *sauté* the spring onions (scallions), garlic and rice for about 5 minutes.

2. Add the herbs, pour over water or the stock and bring to the boil.

3. Season to taste and reduce to a simmer for about 45 minutes in a covered pot.

4. Remove the bay leaves and cook uncovered for a short while should any excess water remain.

ALMOND RICE

Try to use Jordan as opposed to Californian almonds in this recipe, for their extra flavour. You can substitute cashews, whole or broken, or hazels.

Imperial (Metric)
2 cupsful cooked brown rice
½ cupful almonds which have been oven-roasted
1 clove garlic
1 tablespoonful chopped parsley
½ tablespoonful dried marjoram and thyme

American
2½ cupsful cooked brown rice
½ cupful almonds which have been oven-roasted
1 clove garlic
1 tablespoonful chopped parsley
½ tablespoonful dried marjoram and thyme

As soon as the rice has finished cooking, stir in the almonds, crushed garlic and herbs, cover and let stand for ten minutes.

RICE AND CAULIFLOWER

Imperial (Metric)
1½ cupsful brown rice
2 tablespoonsful vegetable oil
3 cupsful boiling water
1 large cauliflower
1 large onion, chopped
1 large tub plain yogurt (cow or
  goat)

American
1⅔ cupsful brown rice
2½ tablespoonsful vegetable oil
3¾ cupsful boiling water
1 large cauliflower
1 large onion, chopped
1 large tub plain yogurt (cow or
  goat)

1. *Sauté* rice in oil for a few minutes in a large, heavy saucepan.

2. Add the boiling water then turn down heat to a gentle simmer.

3. *Sauté* cauliflower florets gently for a few minutes. Add the onion.

4. *Sauté* onion and cauliflower gently for a few minutes more.

5. Lay the vegetables on top of rice and cover with lid.

6. Cook for 45 minutes over gentle heat and then serve with yogurt in side dish.

SPINACH AND RICE

Imperial (Metric)	American
2 tablespoonsful vegetable oil	2½ tablespoonsful vegetable oil
1 small onion, chopped	1 small onion, chopped
4 oz (100g) long grain brown rice	½ cupful long grain brown rice
1 cupful tinned tomatoes	1¼ cupsful tinned tomatoes
1 cupful water or vegetable stock	1¼ cupsful water or vegetable stock
2 lb (1 kilo) spinach, well washed, drained and stalks removed	2 pounds spinach, well washed, drained and stalks removed
4 tablespoonsful chopped parsley	5 tablespoonsful chopped parsley
1 teaspoonful mint	1 teaspoonful mint
1 teaspoonful sea salt	1 teaspoonful sea salt
1 teaspoonful freshly ground black pepper	1 teaspoonful freshly ground black pepper
½ teaspoonful nutmeg	½ teaspoonful nutmeg
1 hard-boiled egg (optional)	1 hard-boiled egg (optional)
1 lemon, cut into wedges	1 lemon, cut into wedges

1. Heat the oil in a heavy-bottomed saucepan, then *sauté* the onion for 5 minutes.

2. Add the rice and cook for a few minutes more, stirring constantly.

3. Add the tomatoes and water or stock.

4. Cover the pan and simmer until the rice is almost cooked (approx. 35 minutes).

5. Uncover the pan and stir in the spinach, parsley and mint with the seasonings.

6. Cook until all the liquid is absorbed, then transfer to a serving dish and garnish with sliced hard-boiled egg and lemon wedges.

MOROCCAN RICE ALICANTINA

Imperial (Metric)	American
3-4 crushed cloves garlic	3-4 crushed cloves garlic
4 tablespoonsful vegetable oil	5 tablespoonsful vegetable oil
3 large green peppers, sliced	3 large green peppers, sliced
1 cupful artichoke hearts	1¼ cupsful artichoke hearts
3 large tomatoes, chopped	3 large tomatoes, chopped
1 cupful green beans, chopped	1¼ cupsful green beans, chopped
1½ cupsful long grain brown rice	1⅔ cupsful long grain brown rice
½ teaspoonful sea salt	½ teaspoonful sea salt
Pinch of freshly ground black pepper	Pinch of freshly ground black pepper
Pinch of turmeric	Pinch of turmeric
3 pints (1½ litres) vegetable stock or water	7½ cupsful vegetable stock or water

1. Fry the garlic in hot oil with the green peppers. Set aside.

2. *Sauté* artichokes, chopped tomatoes and beans.

3. Add rice, seasonings and turmeric.

4. Stir in the stock and cook briskly for 10 minutes, stirring constantly.

5. Simmer gently for approx. another 30 minutes until rice is cooked, then set to one side of the stove and allow to dry out.

6. Stir in the garlic and green pepper mixture and serve warm.

ZEN HASH

This dish was featured on the menu of the Zen Hashery, one of New York's earliest macrobiotic restaurants.

Imperial (Metric)	American
2 lb (1 kilo) courgettes	2 pounds zucchini
1 lb (½ kilo) spinach	1 pound spinach
1 large onion	1 large onion
1 carrot	1 carrot
4 tablespoonsful vegetable oil	5 tablespoonsful vegetable oil
½ cupful real soya sauce	½ cupful real soya sauce
½ cupful pine kernels or cashew nuts	½ cupful pine kernels or cashew nuts
Cooked brown rice	Cooked brown rice

1. Quarter and slice courgettes (zucchini).

2. Coarsely chop spinach and onion and grate carrot.

3. In a large frying pan (skillet), *sauté* onion until golden in colour.

4. Add courgettes (zucchini) and *sauté* until nearly done (about 5 minutes).

5. Add soya sauce and nuts and mix well, then add carrot and spinach and cook for another 3 to 5 minutes until spinach is done. Season to taste.

6. Place brown rice on plates with hollowed out beds in the middle to fill with the vegetable mixture.

7. Garnish with parsley sprigs, carrot sticks or whole radishes (including tops).

STUFFED VINE LEAVES

Imperial (Metric)	American
½ lb (¼ kilo) vine leaves	½ pound vine leaves
¾ cupful cooked brown rice	1 cupful cooked brown rice
½ chopped tomato	½ chopped tomato
¼ cupful chopped pine nuts	¼ cupful chopped pine nuts
½ cupful parsley, finely chopped	½ cupful parsley, finely chopped
2 teaspoonsful dried mint	2 teaspoonsful dried mint
1 teaspoonful sea salt	1 teaspoonful sea salt
1¼ cupsful water or vegetable stock	1½ cupsful water or vegetable stock
4 tablespoonsful lemon juice	5 tablespoonsful lemon juice
3-4 crushed cloves garlic	3-4 crushed cloves garlic

1. Dip vine leaves a few at a time in boiling water.

2. Prepare filling by mixing rice, tomato, pine nuts, parsley, mint, seasoning and ¼ cupful of the water or stock.

3. Place 1 teaspoonful of the mixture in the centre of a leaf. Fold tip of leaf and the stem end of leaf towards centre. Fold sides in toward centre then roll leaf gently to give a torpedo shape.

4. Lay rolled leaves neatly in a pan, and add 1 cupful of the water or stock. Sprinkle with lemon juice and seasoning and cover with a plate to prevent movement.

5. Simmer gently for 1 hour, then drain off the remaining stock and mix with crushed garlic. Pour over vine leaves and simmer for a few more minutes.

6. Serve hot with the sauce or cold sprinkled with lemon juice.

BROWN RICE WITH GRAPES AND PINE NUTS

Imperial (Metric)
2 tablespoonsful olive oil
1 large onion, chopped
2 oz (50g) pine nuts
1½ cupsful long grain brown rice
1½ cupsful boiling vegetable stock
  or water
½ teaspoonful thyme
1 bay leaf
Sea salt and freshly ground black
  pepper
¾ lb (350g) black grapes, peeled,
  halved and seeded

American
2½ tablespoonsful olive oil
1 large onion, chopped
½ cupful pine nuts
1⅔ cupsful long grain brown rice
1⅔ cupsful boiling vegetable stock
  or water
½ teaspoonful thyme
1 bay leaf
Sea salt and freshly ground black
  pepper
¾ pound black grapes, peeled,
  halved and seeded

1. Heat oil in a heavy saucepan, and *sauté* onion until soft and golden.

2. Add pine nuts and cook until they are lightly browned also.

3. Add the rice, stirring well until the grains are well coated with oil.

4. Add the stock, bring to the boil, then add the thyme and bay leaf.

5. Cover the pan and simmer gently until the rice is tender (approx. 45 minutes) and has absorbed the stock. Season with the salt and pepper.

6. Add the grapes. Do not cook any further, but allow the grapes to warm through only.

Note: This is delicious served with a vegetable casserole.

RICE COOKED IN GREEN TEA WITH CHESTNUTS

Imperial (Metric)
2 cupsful short grain brown rice
1 cupful dried chestnuts
1 teaspoonful sea salt
4 cupsful green tea

American
2½ cupsful short grain brown rice
1¼ cupsful dried chestnuts
1 teaspoonful sea salt
5 cupsful green tea

1. Add rice, chestnuts and salt to the tea.

2. Bring to the boil, then simmer (covered) gently for approx. 40 minutes.

6.

BROWN RICE AND SAUCES

In whatever company it is served, boiled or baked brown rice benefits from the addition of some kind of sauce. In its simplest form this may just be a dash of soya sauce or a few spoonsful of the juices from a vegetable dish. Some of the more elaborate sauces practically make a meal on their own when combined with rice.

VEGETABLE SAUCE

Imperial (Metric)	American
1 tablespoonful vegetable oil	1 tablespoonful vegetable oil
1 onion, thinly sliced	1 onion, thinly sliced
1 green pepper, thinly sliced	1 green pepper, thinly sliced
1 carrot, thinly sliced	1 carrot, thinly sliced
3 cloves garlic, finely chopped	3 cloves garlic, finely chopped
¾ cupful water	1 cupful water
3 tablespoonsful real soya sauce	3½ tablespoonsful real soya sauce
1-1½ tablespoonsful *kuzu* powder, dissolved in a little cold water	1-1½ tablespoonsful *kuzu* powder, dissolved in a little cold water
2 teaspoonsful ginger, freshly grated	2 teaspoonsful ginger, freshly grated

1. Heat the oil in a heavy-bottomed pan (skillet) and *sauté* the vegetables and garlic until they are tender.

2. Add the water and the soya sauce and bring to the boil.

3. Stir in the dissolved *kuzu* (if unobtainable, use arrowroot instead) and the ginger and simmer, stirring constantly for about 1 minute or until the sauce thickens and is transparent. (If you cannot get fresh ginger, use powdered instead.)

Note: There are many different vegetables you can use in this sauce. Oriental chefs often use Lotus roots, Daikon (large white radish), Chinese cabbage, mushrooms, bean sprouts, cauliflower or white cabbage.

BASIC ONION SAUCE

Imperial (Metric)	American
3 tablespoonsful chopped onion	3½ tablespoonsful chopped onion
1 clove garlic, crushed	1 clove garlic, crushed
3 tablespoonsful vegetable oil	3½ tablespoonsful vegetable oil
4 tablespoonsful wholewheat flour	5 tablespoonsful wholewheat flour
1½ cupsful water	1⅔ cupsful water
Real soya sauce	Real soya sauce

1. *Sauté* onion and garlic in oil for a few minutes until onions become translucent.

2. Add flour and stir whilst frying for another minute.

3. Add the water slowly, stirring constantly to ensure lumps do not form.

4. When the sauce has thickened, season to taste with soya sauce.

Note: This sauce can benefit from the following additions once you have prepared the basic sauce.

Mustard Sauce
Add 1 teaspoonful of powdered mustard and 1 tablespoonful of lemon juice to the onion sauce.

Dill and Yogurt Sauce
Add 2 teaspoonsful of dried dill (leaves or seeds) and 4 tablespoonsful (5 US) of yogurt to the completed sauce.

Egg Sauce
Add 2 chopped hard-boiled eggs.

ITALIAN SAUCE

Imperial (Metric)	American
2 medium-sized onions, chopped	2 medium-sized onions, chopped
4 cloves garlic, chopped	4 cloves garlic, chopped
2 tablespoonsful vegetable oil	2½ tablespoonsful vegetable oil
1 large carrot, grated	1 large carrot, grated
2 stalks celery, chopped	2 stalks celery, chopped
3 tablespoonsful real soya sauce	3½ tablespoonsful real soya sauce
2 tablespoonsful cider vinegar	2½ tablespoonsful cider vinegar
2 tablespoonsful apple concentrate	2½ tablespoonsful apple concentrate
½ pint (¼ litre) water	1⅓ cupsful water
2 bay leaves	2 bay leaves
1 heaped tablespoonful tomato *purée*	1 heaped tablespoonful tomato paste
1½ teaspoonsful basil	1½ teaspoonsful basil
1 teaspoonful kelp	1 teaspoonful kelp
½ teaspoonful cinnamon	½ teaspoonful cinnamon
1 medium-sized tin tomatoes	1 medium-sized tin tomatoes

1. *Sauté* the onion and garlic in the oil for 5 minutes, add the carrot and celery and cook for a few more minutes.

2. Add the remaining ingredients and simmer gently for 30 minutes.

Note: This is wonderful served over rice. Any leftover sauce is a very tasty addition to the Miso and Rice Soup (page 30).

SWEET AND SOUR SAUCE

Imperial (Metric)	American
1 onion, thinly sliced	1 onion, thinly sliced
½ carrot, chopped finely	½ carrot, chopped finely
1 green pepper, chopped finely	1 green pepper, chopped finely
1 tablespoonful vegetable oil	1 tablespoonful vegetable oil
1 cupful water	1¼ cupsful water
2 tablespoonsful real soya sauce	2½ tablespoonsful real soya sauce
4 teaspoonsful honey	5 teaspoonsful honey
2 teaspoonsful vinegar	2 teaspoonsful vinegar
2 teaspoonsful *kuzu*, dissolved in a little water	2 teaspoonsful *kuzu*, dissolved in a little water

1. Heat a heavy-bottomed pan (skillet) and *sauté* the vegetables in the oil for 5 minutes.

2. Add the water, soya sauce, honey and vinegar and bring to the boil, then simmer gently for another 5 minutes.

3. Stir in the dissolved *kuzu* and cook gently until thickened.

SESAME SAUCE

Imperial (Metric)
1 teaspoonful *kuzu* powder,
  dissolved in a little water
1 cupful water
1 tablespoonful *hatcho miso*
  (soya paste)
1 teaspoonful *tahini* (sesame paste)
1 teaspoonful ginger, freshly grated
  or powdered

American
1 teaspoonful *kuzu* powder,
  dissolved in a little water
1¼ cupsful water
1 tablespoonful *hatcho miso*
  (soya paste)
1 teaspoonful *tahini* (sesame paste)
1 teaspoonful ginger, freshly grated
  or powdered

1. Add the *kuzu* powder (ready dissolved) to the cupful of water in a saucepan. Bring to the boil and then simmer for a few minutes until the sauce has thickened.

2. Mix in the remaining ingredients and simmer for a few minutes more.

Note: This is delicious served over steamed cauliflower, asparagus, potatoes, broccoli or any *sautéd* vegetables.

APPLE DESSERT SAUCE

Imperial (Metric)
1½ tablespoonsful *kuzu*
1 tablespoonful honey
1 cupful apple concentrate
½ cupful water
1 tablespoonful lemon juice
¼ teaspoonful nutmeg

American
1½ tablespoonsful *kuzu*
1 tablespoonful honey
1¼ cupsful apple concentrate
½ cupful water
1 tablespoonful lemon juice
¼ teaspoonful nutmeg

1. Combine the *kuzu*, honey and half of the apple concentrate in a pan, mixing well.

2. Stir in the remaining apple juice and water.

3. Bring to the boil, stirring constantly until the sauce has thickened.

4. Stir in the lemon juice and nutmeg and serve hot or cold over fruits or rice pudding.

is for apple

MISO SAUCE

Imperial (Metric)	American
8 tablespoonsful *tahini* (sesame paste)	10 tablespoonsful *tahini* (sesame paste)
2 tablespoonsful *miso* — any variety (preferably *genmai miso*)	2½ tablespoonsful *miso* — any variety (preferably *genmai miso*)
1¾ cupsful water	2 cupsful water
1½ teaspoonful grated orange peel	1½ teaspoonsful grated orange peel

1. Mix *tahini, miso* and water together and cook in a saucepan on a low flame for 10 to 15 minutes.

2. Add orange peel when sauce is done.

Note: For a delicious spread for bread and sandwiches simply use less water, mix all the ingredients to a buttery paste and do not cook.

TAMARI SAUCE

You can substitute *shoyu* or other good quality soya sauce for *tamari* in this recipe. The sauce is also good with most cooked green vegetables.

Imperial (Metric)
4 tablespoonsful *tamari*
2 tablespoonsful vegetable oil
¼ cupful water
1 tablespoonful arrowroot or *kuzu* (Japanese arrowroot)

American
5 tablespoonsful *tamari*
2½ tablespoonsful vegetable oil
¼ cupful water
1 tablespoonful arrowroot or *kuzu* (Japanese arrowroot)

1. Mix *tamari* and oil in a small saucepan and bring to the boil.

2. Add water and boil for 5 minutes.

3. Meanwhile, dissolve arrowroot in 2 tablespoonsful of water and add this mixture to the boiling liquid mixture. Stir constantly until the sauce thickens.

RAISIN SAUCE

Raisin sauce is not only good with rice (e.g. when serving curries or to stimulate the interest of children), but also goes well over vegetables such as steamed carrots. A bit of zest (grated lemon peel) can be added if desired.

Imperial (Metric)	American
3 tablespoonsful vegetable oil	3½ tablespoonsful vegetable oil
3 tablespoonsful wholewheat flour	3½ tablespoonsful wholewheat flour
1 cupful fresh apple juice or apple juice concentrate rediluted with 6 parts water	1¼ cupsful fresh apple juice or apple juice concentrate rediluted with 6 parts water
1 cupful chopped raisins or whole currants	1¼ cupsful chopped raisins or whole currants
½ teaspoonful sea salt	½ teaspoonful sea salt

1. Heat the oil in a saucepan, then add the flour and roast for a minute, stirring constantly.

2. Slowly add the apple juice, taking care lumps do not form. Cook slowly, stirring frequently until the sauce has thickened.

3. Add raisins and simmer gently for 4 minutes, stirring regularly to prevent sticking.

MUSHROOM SAUCE

Imperial (Metric)
¼ cupful chopped mushrooms
3 tablespoonsful vegetable oil
3 tablespoonsful wholewheat flour
1 cupful water (or milk in some
   proportion for a richer sauce)
2 teaspoonsful real soya sauce

American
¼ cupful chopped mushrooms
3½ tablespoonsful vegetable oil
3½ tablespoonsful wholewheat flour
1¼ cupful water (or milk in some
   proportion for a richer sauce)
2 teaspoonsful real soya sauce

1. *Sauté* mushrooms in oil for a few minutes, then add the flour.

2. Cook for a further minute, stirring continuously.

3. Slowly add the water, stirring constantly, adding more water carefully to avoid lumps forming.

4. When the sauce has thickened, add soya sauce to taste.

Note: You can adjust the thickness of this sauce by increasing the amount of flour and oil used.

SAVOURY THICKENED TAMARI

This is a dipping sauce and is very popular in Japan. It is delicious used as a dip for finely slivered carrots, spring onions (scallions), celery etc. Also poured over cooked vegetables, tofu, or cooked brown rice.

Imperial (Metric)	American
1 teaspoonful sesame oil	1 teaspoonful sesame oil
¼ cupful real soya sauce	¼ cupful real soya sauce
¼ cupful water	¼ cupful water
1½ tablespoonsful *kuzu* (dissolved in a little water)	1½ tablespoonsful *kuzu* (dissolved in a little water)

1. Heat a small pan and coat with the oil, then add the soya sauce and bring to the boil.

2. Add the water and dissolved *kuzu*, bring to the boil and then simmer gently, stirring constantly until the sauce is thickened.

TOMATO SAUCE
Serve this in the middle of a bowl of rice.

Imperial (Metric)
3 tablespoonsful olive oil
2 medium-sized onions, chopped
2 stalks celery, chopped
5 cloves garlic, crushed
¼ teaspoonful thyme
1 teaspoonful real soya sauce
1 tablespoonful cider vinegar
3 umeboshi plums, pitted
1 can tomato *purée* or *purée* of 4
  peeled and seeded tomatoes

American
3½ tablespoonsful olive oil
2 medium-sized onions, chopped
2 stalks celery, chopped
5 cloves garlic, crushed
¼ teaspoonful thyme
1 teaspoonful real soya sauce
1 tablespoonful cider vinegar
3 umeboshi plums, pitted
1 can tomato paste or sauce of 4
  peeled and seeded tomatoes

1. *Sauté* vegetables, garlic, thyme, soya sauce, vinegar and plums in the oil.

2. Add *purée* (paste) diluted with equal quantity of water. Simmer gently for 15 minutes.

PESTO SAUCE

Imperial (Metric)	American
1 large bunch of fresh basil	1 large bunch of fresh basil
4 cloves garlic	4 cloves garlic
Pinch of sea salt	Pinch of sea salt
½ cupful pine nuts	½ cupful pine nuts
½ cupful grated Parmesan cheese	½ cupful grated Parmesan cheese
4 tablespoonsful olive oil	5 tablespoonsful olive oil

1. Pound the basil leaves (removing the stalks) in a mortar with garlic, salt and pine nuts. Add the cheese.

2. When the pesto is a thick *purée* (paste), add the olive oil a little at a time, stirring constantly.

Note: The finished sauce should have the consistency of a creamed butter. If it is impossible to get fresh basil, parsley may be used instead and walnuts (English walnuts) instead of pine nuts, but it will of course have a completely different flavour, although still delicious.

CAULIFLOWER SAUCE

Imperial (Metric)	American
1 cauliflower	1 cauliflower
2 medium-sized onions, chopped	2 medium-sized onions, chopped
4 tablespoonsful vegetable oil	5 tablespoonsful vegetable oil
3 tablespoonsful wholewheat flour	3½ tablespoonsful wholewheat flour
1 teaspoonful sea salt	1 teaspoonful sea salt
1 teaspoonful *tamari*	1 teaspoonful *tamari*

1. Clean cauliflower and lightly cook in boiling water. Drain and reserve 1 pint (½ litre/2½ cupsful) liquid.

2. *Sauté* onions in the oil and when transparent stir in the flour.

3. Cook lightly for a minute or two and then add the cauliflower stock. Stir until the sauce comes to the boil.

4. Add the cauliflower, well broken up. Season with salt and *tamari*, then turn down to a very gentle heat and cook slowly for 20 minutes. Serve over brown rice or any grain.

7.

SALADS

Salads based on brown rice are particularly ideal in summer but they are delicious at any season. Apart from being a useful way of preparing leftover cooked rice, salads also make a welcome change from packed lunches when cheese sandwiches have begun to pall.

MIXED BEAN SALAD

Imperial (Metric)	American
4 oz (100g) dried kidney beans	¾ cupful dried kidney beans
4 oz (100g) chick peas	½ cupful garbanzo beans
4 oz (100g) haricot beans	½ cupful navy beans
4 oz (100g) brown rice, cooked	¾ cupful brown rice, cooked
1 lb (½ kilo) sliced green beans	1 pound sliced green beans
2 onions	2 onions

Vinaigrette:

Imperial (Metric)	American
1 cupful olive oil	1¼ cupsful olive oil
½ cupful wine vinegar	½ cupful wine vinegar
1 clove garlic, crushed	1 clove garlic, crushed
Sea salt and freshly ground black pepper	Sea salt and freshly ground black pepper
Mustard	Mustard

1. Soak pulses overnight, then cook for 1½-2 hours — separately if convenient.

2. Cook green beans in salted water until tender but not too soft.

3. Slice onions into rings.

4. Drain beans and green beans as well.

5. Mix all the salad ingredients in a bowl and pour on vinaigrette. Set aside to cool.

BROWN RICE AND LENTIL SALAD

This delicious salad is at its best with *lentilles de Puy,* the delicious small green lentils from France. There is a Canadian lentil that is similar, and of course you can use the usual greenish grey 'continental' lentils with good results.

Imperial (Metric)	American
1 cupful lentils	1¼ cupsful lentils
1 cupful brown rice	1¼ cupsful brown rice
1 cupful sliced mushrooms	1¼ cupsful sliced mushrooms
½ cupful chopped spring onions	½ cupful chopped scallions
½ green pepper, chopped	½ green pepper, chopped
1 heaped tablespoonful chopped walnuts	1 heaped tablespoonful chopped English walnuts
½ cupful chopped and peeled cucumber	½ cupful chopped and peeled cucumber
3 tablespoonsful chopped parsley	3½ tablespoonsful chopped parsley

Dressing:

Imperial (Metric)	American
5 tablespoonsful vegetable oil	6 tablespoonsful vegetable oil
5 tablespoonsful cider vinegar	6 tablespoonsful cider vinegar
1 teaspoonful mustard powder	1 teaspoonful mustard powder
2 cloves garlic, crushed	2 cloves garlic, crushed
½ teaspoonful freshly ground black pepper	½ teaspoonful freshly ground black pepper
1 teaspoonful real soya sauce	1 teaspoonful real soya sauce

1. Cook the lentils in four parts boiling water until soft (about ¾ hour) without salt.

2. Cook the rice in lightly salted water until done.

3. Combine lentils and rice and pour the salad dressing over this mixture while it is still warm. Set aside to cool.

4. Add the remaining ingredients and garnish with parsley sprigs or slices of tomato or pimento.

RICE SALAD

Imperial (Metric)
½ lb (¼ kilo) brown rice
½ lb (¼ kilo) tomatoes
½ red pepper
2 sticks celery

American
1 cupful brown rice
3 medium-sized tomatoes
½ red pepper
2 sticks celery

Dressing 1:

Imperial (Metric)
Juice of 1 lemon
½ teaspoonful paprika
2 tablespoonsful chopped parsley
Sea salt and freshly ground black
   pepper
4 tablespoonsful olive oil

American
Juice of 1 lemon
½ teaspoonful paprika
2½ tablespoonsful chopped parsley
Sea salt and freshly ground black
   pepper
5 tablespoonsful olive oil

Dressing 2:

Imperial (Metric)
¼ pint (150ml) plain yogurt
Sea salt and freshly ground black
   pepper
Mustard
1 teaspoonful real soya sauce
1 clove garlic, crushed
Pinch of cayenne pepper

American
⅔ cupful plain yogurt
Sea salt and freshly ground black
   pepper
Mustard
1 teaspoonful real soya sauce
1 clove garlic, crushed
Pinch of cayenne pepper

1. Cook rice, skin and chop tomatoes and finely chop pepper and celery sticks.

2. Mix dressing ingredients (both).

3. Stir rice and vegetables into dressing 1 and press into mould.

4. Refrigerate for 12 hours, then turn out onto a bed of lettuce and serve with dressing 2.

PARADISE SALAD

Imperial (Metric)
3 cupsful cooked brown rice —
  long and short grain mixed
4 sticks celery, diced
2 oz (50g) raisins
Fresh herbs, chopped
2 oz (50g) grapes
4 tomatoes, halved
4 hard-boiled eggs, halved
1 cupful mayonnaise
8 black olives

American
3¾ cupsful cooked brown rice —
  long and short grain mixed
4 sticks celery, diced
⅓ cupful raisins
Fresh herbs, chopped
½ cupful grapes
4 tomatoes, halved
4 hard-boiled eggs, halved
1¼ cupful mayonnaise
8 black olives

1. Mix the cooked rice with the celery, raisins, any fresh herbs available and grapes.

2. Place in a mould in the middle of a serving dish, arranging the halves of tomato and egg alternately.

3. Put a teaspoonful of mayonnaise onto each egg half and an olive onto each tomato half.

ALMOND AND RICE SALAD

Imperial (Metric)
2 cupsful cooked brown rice
¼ teaspoonful curry powder
½ cupful mayonnaise
½ cupful chopped celery
½ cupful almonds, toasted and
  slivered

American
2½ cupsful cooked brown rice
¼ teaspoonful curry powder
½ cupful mayonnaise
½ cupful chopped celery
½ cupful almonds, toasted and
  slivered

1. Chill the rice and stir in the remaining ingredients.

2. Serve at once.

ADZUKI BEAN SALAD

Imperial (Metric)	American
4 oz (100g) adzuki beans	½ cupful adzuki beans
2 cupsful cooked brown rice	2½ cupsful cooked brown rice
1 large green pepper, chopped and de-seeded	1 large green pepper, chopped and de-seeded
2 sticks celery, finely chopped	2 sticks celery, finely chopped
½ cucumber, diced	½ cucumber, diced
6 spring onions, chopped	6 scallions, chopped

Dressing:

Imperial (Metric)	American
4 tablespoonsful olive oil	5 tablespoonsful olive oil
1 tablespoonful wine vinegar	1 tablespoonful wine vinegar
1 clove garlic, crushed	1 clove garlic, crushed
1 teaspoonful mustard	1 teaspoonful mustard
1 teaspoonful sea salt	1 teaspoonful sea salt
2 tablespoonsful parsley, finely chopped	2½ tablespoonsful parsley, finely chopped
2 tablespoonsful celery, finely chopped	2½ tablespoonsful celery, finely chopped
Freshly ground black pepper	Freshly ground black pepper

1. Soak beans overnight, then cook until tender (about an hour). Do *not* add salt.

2. Mix the dressing in a salad bowl. Add the cooked rice and beans straight into the dressing. Turn lightly with a fork and leave to cool.

3. Mix in the chopped vegetables. Taste and season with sea salt and freshly ground black pepper.

IRISH SALAD

Imperial (Metric)
2 leeks, well cleaned and finely shredded
4 sticks celery, finely chopped
2 medium-sized carrots, peeled and grated
1 cupful cooked brown rice

American
2 leeks, well cleaned and finely shredded
4 sticks celery, finely chopped
2 medium-sized carrots, peeled and grated
1 cupful cooked brown rice

Dressing:

Imperial (Metric)
3 tablespoonsful olive oil
1 tablespoonful wine vinegar
1 clove garlic, crushed
1/2 teaspoonful mustard
Sea salt and freshly ground black pepper
Finely chopped parsley
12 black olives

American
3 1/2 tablespoonsful olive oil
1 tablespoonful wine vinegar
1 clove garlic, crushed
1/2 teaspoonful mustard
Sea salt and freshly ground black pepper
Finely chopped parsley
12 black olives

1. Mix together vegetables and rice in a salad bowl.

2. Mix dressing and add to vegetables. Garnish with the parsley and olives.

3. Serve with warmed wholewheat bread.

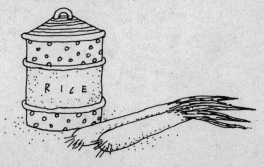

GREEK HOT RICE SALAD

Imperial (Metric)
1 teaspoonful sea salt
¼ teaspoonful freshly ground black pepper
1 onion, finely chopped
2 cupsful hot brown rice, cooked
¼ cupful olive oil
1 tablespoonful lemon juice
Oregano
Parsley sprigs and ripe olives for garnishing

American
1 teaspoonful sea salt
¼ teaspoonful freshly ground black pepper
1 onion, finely chopped
2½ cupsful hot brown rice, cooked
¼ cupful olive oil
1 tablespoonful lemon juice
Oregano
Parsley sprigs and ripe olives for garnishing

1. Add salt, pepper and onion to the hot rice.

2. Mix together the oil and lemon juice and pour over the rice.

3. Sprinkle with oregano and toss lightly. Garnish and serve at once.

PINK RICE SALAD

Imperial (Metric)
1 cupful finely chopped celery
1 cupful finely chopped parsley
1 cupful pre-cooked, diced and
   cooled beetroot
3 cupsful long grain brown rice
1 cupful pre-cooked, diced and
   cooled carrots

American
1¼ cupsful finely chopped celery
1¼ cupsful finely chopped parsley
1¼ cupsful pre-cooked, diced and
   cooled beet
3¾ cupsful long grain brown rice
1¼ cupsful pre-cooked, diced and
   cooled carrots

Dressing:

Imperial (Metric)
4 tablespoonsful olive oil
1 tablespoonful cider vinegar or
   lemon juice
Sea salt and freshly ground black
   pepper
1 tablespoonful *tahini*

American
5 tablespoonsful olive oil
1 tablespoonful cider vinegar or
   lemon juice
Sea salt and freshly ground black
   pepper
1 tablespoonful *tahini*

1. Mix together the salad ingredients.

2. Mix together the dressing ingredients, then pour over the salad.

3. Mix well until beetroot (beet) juice stains rice pink, taking care
   salad does not become mushy.

8.

RISOTTOS, CASSEROLES AND RISSOLES

AUTUMN RISOTTO

Imperial (Metric)
4 tablespoonsful olive oil
1 large onion, chopped
2 potatoes, diced
2 carrots, diced
3 courgettes, sliced across
½ lb (¼ kilo) string or green beans, chopped
4 oz (100g) cabbage, shredded
2 cupsful brown rice
2 cupsful vegetable stock
2 cupsful tomato juice
2 large cloves garlic, crushed
Sea salt and freshly ground black pepper
1 cupful Parmesan cheese
2 tablespoonsful parsley, chopped

American
5 tablespoonsful olive oil
1 large onion, chopped
2 potatoes, diced
2 carrots, diced
3 zucchini, sliced across
½ pound string or green beans, chopped
4 ounces cabbage, shredded
2½ cupsful brown rice
2½ cupsful vegetable stock
2½ cupsful tomato juice
2 large cloves garlic, crushed
Sea salt and freshly ground black pepper
1¼ cupsful Parmesan cheese
2½ tablespoonsful parsley, chopped

1. Heat oil until hot in heavy casserole.

2. Add all the vegetables, stirring constantly until they begin to soften.

3. Add the rice, stir and cook for a further few minutes before adding the stock and tomato juice.

4. Now add the garlic and season with salt and pepper.

5. Bring to simmering point, then transfer uncovered to the oven for 35 minutes at 350°F/180°C (Gas Mark 4).

6. Remove from oven, sprinkle with Parmesan and parsley and leave to stand for 10 minutes in a warm place before serving.

CASHEW RISOTTO

Imperial (Metric)	American
1/2 lemon	1/2 lemon
2 cupsful cooked brown rice	2 1/2 cupsful cooked brown rice
2 tomatoes, peeled and seeded	2 tomatoes, peeled and seeded
2 hard-boiled eggs, chopped	2 hard-boiled eggs, chopped
2 tablespoonsful parsley, chopped	2 1/2 tablespoonsful parsley, chopped
Real soya sauce	Real soya sauce
Wholewheat breadcrumbs	Wholewheat breadcrumbs
3-4 tablespoonsful grated cheese	3 1/2-5 tablespoonsful grated cheese

1. Finely grate the lemon rind and juice the lemon.

2. Mix the juice, rind, rice, nuts, tomatoes, eggs and parsley, season with soya sauce.

3. Place mixture in an oiled casserole dish. Sprinkle top with mixed breadcrumbs and cheese.

4. Bake at 300°F/150°C (Gas Mark 2) for 20-25 minutes.

SPRING RISOTTO

Imperial (Metric)	American
4 tablespoonsful olive oil	5 tablespoonsful olive oil
1 onion, chopped	1 onion, chopped
2 cupsful long grain brown rice	2½ cupsful long grain brown rice
3½ cupsful boiling water	4 cupsful boiling water
1 small cauliflower	1 small cauliflower
1 lb (½ kilo) broccoli (heads only)	1 pound broccoli (heads only)
2 leeks, chopped	2 leeks, chopped
Sea salt, freshly ground black pepper and cayenne	Sea salt, freshly ground black pepper and cayenne
½ lb (¼ kilo) spinach, chopped	½ pound spinach, chopped
4 oz (100g) strong Cheddar cheese, grated	1 cupful strong Cheddar cheese, grated
4 spring onions, finely chopped	4 scallions, finely chopped

1. Heat half the oil in a heavy saucepan and *sauté* onion for 5 minutes.

2. Add the rice, stirring well to coat all the grains in oil, then add the boiling water and a pinch of sea salt. Cover and simmer for 40 minutes.

3. Heat the remaining oil in a heavy casserole. *Sauté* the cauliflower florets, broccoli, leeks and seasonings together, stirring gently for about 10 minutes.

4. Add the spinach, stirring for a few minutes whilst it reduces in size.

5. Add the cooked rice and half the cheese, sprinkle the remaining cheese and the cayenne on top and grill until the cheese is melted and golden.

6. Sprinkle with the spring onions (scallions) and serve.

SUNSHINE RISOTTO

This delicious dish combines the nutty flavour of toasted seeds with the sweetness of dried fruits to give an exotic flavour and a satisfying meal. Dried fruits featured heavily in the cuisine of the Middle Ages in conjunction with game and cereal dishes. The traditional English breakfast of 'frumenty' was made with boiled wheat, a little milk and 'raisins of Corinth' (as currants were known in their early days when they were the most commonly available dried vine fruit). Nowadays fruit packers often treat raisins, sultanas (golden seedless raisins) and currants with paraffin oil to speed up the rate at which they can be packed, but this is undesirable as paraffin can inhibit the digestive system's ability to absorb the nutritive elements in your food. Dried fruit which has been rewashed and cleaned and repacked, unoiled, is available for a few pence extra per pound at many natural food stores and other outlets.

Imperial (Metric)	American
1 carrot, diced	1 carrot, diced
2 onions, chopped	2 onions, chopped
3 stalks celery, chopped	3 stalks celery, chopped
Vegetable oil	Vegetable oil
1 cupful sunflower seeds	1¼ cupful sunflower seeds
3 cupsful cooked long grain brown rice	3¾ cupsful cooked long grain brown rice
½ cupful raisins	½ cupful raisins
½ cupful currants	½ cupful currants
1½ cupsful grated cheese (double Gloucester or Leicester)	1⅔ cupsful grated cheese (double Gloucester or Leicester)
1 teaspoonful *tamari* soya sauce	1 teaspoonful *tamari* soya sauce

1. *Sauté* the vegetables in oil until the onions are soft and translucent.

2. Toast the seeds in the oven at 350°F/180°C (Gas Mark 4) for 7 to 8 minutes. Remove from oven and *sauté* with the vegetables.

3. Add rice, raisins and currants, adding a little water if needed to prevent sticking while it heats up. Put the whole mixture into a casserole and mix with half a cupful of the cheese and *tamari*.

4. Sprinkle the remaining cheese over the top and cover. Bake for about 10 minutes at 350°F/180°C (Gas Mark 4) until the cheese is melted and just crisping at the edges of the dish.

STUFFED CABBAGE LEAVES

Imperial (Metric)	American
1 large onion, chopped	1 large onion, chopped
1 carrot, finely chopped	1 carrot, finely chopped
1 tablespoonful vegetable oil	1 tablespoonful vegetable oil
1½ cupsful cooked short grain brown rice	1⅔ cupsful cooked short grain brown rice
1½ cupsful cooked buckwheat	1⅔ cupsful cookd buckwheat
Real soya sauce	Real soya sauce
1 cupful grated cheese	1¼ cupsful grated cheese
1 cabbage	1 cabbage

1. *Sauté* the onion and carrot in oil and mix with the cooked brown rice and buckwheat.

2. Season with soya sauce. (You may add an egg at this stage to bind the filling if desired.) Stir in the grated cheese.

3. Boil the head of cabbage in water for 4 to 5 minutes, then remove from the water and drain. Peel off the outer leaves slowly, taking care not to tear them.

4. Place 3 tablespoonsful of filling on each leaf, and roll it up, tucking in the ends as soon as one complete turn is made.

5. Oil an ovenproof casserole dish and place the rolls in it side by side.

6. Cover the bottom of the dish with a little water and cover with lid.

7. Bake for 25 minutes in a medium oven at about 350°F/180°C (Gas Mark 4).

Note: The rolls should hold together when cooked and can be eaten hot or cold.

PEANUT RICE SUPREME

This recipe is derived from one produced by the Georgia Peanut Commission, a body devoted to the theory that if everyone ate more peanuts the world would be free of wars, pestilence, famine and halitosis. From their recipes we tried and enjoyed this one.

Imperial (Metric)	American
1 large onion, chopped	1 large onion, chopped
2 cupsful celery, chopped	2½ cupsful celery, chopped
3 tablespoonsful groundnut oil	3½ tablespoonsful groundnut oil
1 cupful peanuts, chopped finely	1¼ cupsful peanuts, chopped finely
3 cupsful cooked long grain brown rice	3¾ cupsful cooked long grain brown rice
1 lb (½ kilo) cottage cheese	2 cupsful cottage cheese
1 cupful diced cooked carrots	1¼ cupsful diced cooked carrots
⅓ cupful peanut butter (old-fashioned style)	⅓ cupful peanut butter (old-fashioned style)
4 eggs, beaten	4 eggs, beaten
1 tablespoonful real soya sauce	1 tablespoonful real soya sauce

1. *Sauté* onion and celery in oil until onion is soft. Add all remaining ingredients and blend together well.

2. Place mixture in a casserole dish, well oiled (or lined with oiled foil).

3. Bake at 375°F/190°C (Gas Mark 5) for at least an hour.

4. Unmould the baked loaf, which should have set, onto a serving platter, removing foil. Serve with mushroom or béchamel sauce.

BROWN RICE TRAY KIBBEH

Basic Shell:

Imperial (Metric)	American
1 medium-sized onion, finely chopped	1 medium-sized onion, finely chopped
2 cupsful bulgur, soaked	2½ cupsful bulgur, soaked
2 cupsful cooked brown rice	2½ cupsful cooked brown rice
1 tablespoonful vegetable oil	1 tablespoonful vegetable oil
1 teaspoonful sea salt	1 teaspoonful sea salt
1 teaspoonful freshly ground black pepper	1 teaspoonful freshly ground black pepper

Filling:

Imperial (Metric)	American
1 large onion, finely sliced	1 large onion, finely sliced
2 cloves garlic, finely sliced	2 cloves garlic, finely sliced
1 tablespoonful vegetable oil	1 tablespoonful vegetable oil
½ lb (¼ kilo) pine nuts	1½ cupsful pine nuts
1 teaspoonful sea salt	1 tablespoonful sea salt
1 teaspoonful freshly ground black pepper	1 teaspoonful freshly ground black pepper
1 teaspoonful allspice	1 teaspoonful allspice
2 tablespoonsful finely chopped parsley	2½ tablespoonsful finely chopped parsley

1. Although traditionally this mix should be pounded by hand until smooth, I use my blender! Mix all the ingredients for the basic shell together in a bowl and feed a small amount at a time into the blender, adding a little water if necessary. Blend until smooth and 'sticky', removing each batch into another bowl to avoid jamming the machine.

2. *Sauté* the onion and garlic for the filling, then add the pine nuts, seasonings and parsley. Cook together for 5 minutes.

3. Oil a shallow pan approx. 8 × 12 × 2 in. (20 × 30 × 50cm) deep.

4. Put a layer of the shell into the bottom of the pan, cover with all the filling and top with the remaining shell.

5. Bake in a moderate oven for 30 minutes until crisp and golden on top.

ONIONS FARCI

The amount of rice used in this recipe depends upon the internal
volume of the onions you are stuffing.

Imperial (Metric)	American
4 large onions with outer brown skin removed	4 large onions with outer brown skin removed
3 tablespoonsful vegetable oil	3½ tablespoonsful vegetable oil
4 oz (100g) chopped mushrooms	1½ cupsful chopped mushrooms
1½ cupsful cooked brown rice (approx.)	1⅔ cupsful cooked brown rice (approx.)
4 oz (100g) double Gloucester cheese, grated	1 cupful double Gloucester cheese, grated
1 tablespoonful real soya sauce	1 tablespoonful real soya sauce
1 teaspoonful thyme	1 teaspoonful thyme
Freshly ground black pepper	Freshly ground black pepper

1. Cook the onions in boiling water until tender, at least for half
    an hour. Drain.

2. Slice off tops and scoop out centres, leaving an outer shell about
    half an inch thick.

3. Chop the onion centres and tops. *Sauté* half the chopped onion
    in oil with the mushrooms for four minutes.

4. Add the rice, half the grated cheese and the seasonings. Stir and
    fry another few minutes.

5. Cover the base of a casserole dish with the rest of the chopped
    onion and a little water.

6. Fill the onion shells with the stuffing mixture, covering with the
    remaining cheese.

7. Bake for half to three-quarters of an hour at 350°F/180°C (Gas
    Mark 4) or until onions are golden in colour.

RICE, RYE AND VEGETABLE PIE

Imperial (Metric)	American
1 cupful carrots	1¼ cupsful carrots
1 cupful parsnips	1¼ cupsful parsnips
1 cupful cabbage	1¼ cupsful cabbage
Tamari soya sauce	*Tamari* soya sauce
1 teaspoonful arrowroot	1 teaspoonful arrowroot
2 cupsful cooked brown rice and rye mixed	2½ cupsful cooked brown rice and rye mixed
1 cupful grated cheese	1¼ cupsful grated cheese
Wholemeal pastry to line pie dish and cover	Wholemeal pastry to line pie dish and cover

1. *Sauté* carrots, parsnips and cabbage, then cover, adding a cupful of water and simmer for 15 minutes.

2. Season with *tamari* and thicken by stirring in a teaspoonful of arrowroot mixed to a smooth paste with water.

3. Add the rice, rye and grated cheese.

4. Line pie dish with pastry, fill with mixture and cover with lid.

5. Bake in a moderate oven until pastry is cooked.

STUFFED MARROW

Imperial (Metric)	American
1 medium-sized marrow	1 medium-sized summer squash
1 medium-sized onion, finely chopped	1 medium-sized onion, finely chopped
2 cloves garlic, finely chopped	2 cloves garlic, finely chopped
1 tablespoonful vegetable oil	1 tablespoonful vegetable oil
2 cupsful cooked brown rice	2 cupsful cooked brown rice
2 cupsful buckwheat groats	2 cupsful buckwheat groats
4 oz (100g) chopped hazelnuts	¾ cupful chopped hazelnuts
1 medium-sized tin tomatoes	1 medium-sized tin tomatoes
1 tablespoonful marjoram	1 tablespoonful marjoram
1 teaspoonful sea salt	1 teaspoonful sea salt
1 teaspoonful freshly ground black pepper	1 teaspoonful freshly ground black pepper
1 cupful water	1¼ cupsful water
2 cupsful grated Cheddar cheese	2½ cupsful grated Cheddar cheese
Pinch of cayenne	Pinch of cayenne

1. Cut the marrow in half lengthways and scoop out the seeds. Lay the halves side by side in an ovenproof dish lined with sufficient tin foil to wrap over the top before baking.

2. *Sauté* the onion and garlic for 5 minutes.

3. Stir in the rice and buckwheat, mixing them together well.

4. Add all the other ingredients with the exception of the cheese and cayenne and cook for a few minutes.

5. Spoon the mixture into the hollowed out sections of the marrow (summer squash). (I often sprinkle the top with grated cheese and cayenne but this is optional.)

6. Bring the foil over the top and cook in a moderate oven for 1 hour or until the marrow is well cooked and soft.

CARROT AND WILD RICE CASSEROLE

Imperial (Metric)
1 large onion, chopped
1 tablespoonful vegetable oil
½ lb (¼ kilo) mix of wild rice and
    long grain brown rice, cooked
2 large carrots, grated
1 tablespoonful *tahini*
1 egg, lightly beaten
1 teaspoonful sea salt

American
1 large onion, chopped
1 tablespoonful vegetable oil
1 cupful mix of wild rice and long
    grain brown rice, cooked
2 large carrots, grated
1 tablespoonful *tahini*
1 egg, lightly beaten
1 teaspoonful sea salt

1. *Sauté* the onion in the oil for 5 minutes.

2. Add the rice and carrot, stir well and cook for another few minutes.

3. Combine the *tahini*, egg and salt and stir into the rice mixture.

4. Turn the mix into a well oiled casserole dish and bake covered for 30 minutes at 350°F/180°C (Gas Mark 4).

TASTY CASSEROLE

Imperial (Metric)	American
2 onions, chopped	2 onions, chopped
2 tablespoonsful lemon juice	2½ tablespoonsful lemon juice
2 cupsful long grain brown rice	2½ cupsful long grain brown rice
1 tablespoonful curry powder	1 tablespoonful curry powder
1 red pepper, chopped	1 red pepper, chopped
1 green pepper, chopped	1 green pepper, chopped
4 oz (100g) mushrooms, chopped	2 cupsful mushrooms, chopped
1 carrot, chopped	1 carrot, chopped
4 oz (100g) peas	⅔ cupful peas
1 teaspoonful freshly ground black pepper	1 teaspoonful freshly ground black pepper
1 pint (½ litre) vegetable stock, boiling	2½ cupsful vegetable stock, boiling

1. Gently cook the onions in lemon juice.

2. Add the rice and curry powder and stir over heat for a few minutes.

3. Put rice mixture in a casserole dish and add the peppers, mushrooms, carrot, peas and black pepper.

4. Add the stock, stir well and cover. Bake at 350°F/180°C (Gas Mark 4) for one hour.

CASSEROLE VERT

Imperial (Metric)	American
1 chopped onion	1 chopped onion
2 cloves garlic, crushed	2 cloves garlic, crushed
Vegetable oil	Vegetable oil
2 cupsful cooked brown rice	2½ cupsful cooked brown rice
¾ cupful grated Cheddar cheese	1 cupful grated Cheddar cheese
2 beaten eggs	2 beaten eggs
2 cupsful milk	2½ cupsful milk
1 tablespoonful real soya sauce	1 tablespoonful real soya sauce
½ cupful chopped parsley	½ cupful chopped parsley

1. *Sauté* the onion and garlic in oil until the onions are soft.

2. Mix remaining ingredients together and add the onions and garlic.

3. Pour into a casserole dish and bake at 350°F/180°C (Gas Mark 4) for at least half an hour or until it has set.

RICE RISSOLES

Imperial (Metric)	American
3 cupsful cooked brown rice	3¾ cupsful cooked brown rice
¼ cupful finely chopped parsley	¼ cupful finely chopped parsley
Pinch of sea salt	Pinch of sea salt
1 cupful *sautéd* onions	1¼ cupsful *sautéd* onions
½ cupful roasted sunflower seeds	½ cupful roasted sunflower seeds
1 tablespoonful vegetable oil	1 tablespoonful vegetable oil
3 chopped spring onions	3 chopped scallions
1 cupful béchamel sauce	1¼ cupsful béchamel sauce
Plain wholewheat flour	Plain wholewheat flour

1. Combine the ingredients, using the béchamel sauce to bind.

2. Shape into patties, using the flour, and fry in pan.

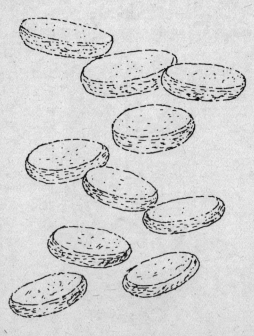

RICE CROQUETTES

Imperial (Metric)	American
1 chopped onion	1 chopped onion
2 cloves garlic, crushed	2 cloves garlic, crushed
3 cupsful cooked short grain brown rice	3¾ cupsful cooked short grain brown rice
½ cupful grated Cheddar cheese	½ cupful grated Cheddar cheese
2 tablespoonsful wholewheat flour	2½ tablespoonsful wholewheat flour
1 beaten egg	1 beaten egg
Wholewheat breadcrumbs or bran	Wholewheat breadcrumbs or bran

1. *Sauté* the onion and garlic until golden, then mix with the cooked rice and grated cheese.

2. Mix with flour to a consistency which can be shaped into small patties.

3. Dip into beaten egg, dredge in breadcrumbs or bran (or a mixture of the two).

4. Bake at 350°F/180°C (Gas Mark 4) for half an hour and serve with béchamel or *tamari* soya sauce.

BROWN RICE KIBBEH

Imperial (Metric)	American
2½ cupsful pre-soaked bulgur	3¼ cupsful pre-soaked bulgur
2 cupsful cooked brown rice	2½ cupsful cooked brown rice
1½ teaspoonsful sea salt	1½ teaspoonsful sea salt
1 cupful hot water	1¼ cupsful hot water
¼ cupful vegetable oil	¼ cupful vegetable oil
1 onion, finely chopped	1 onion, finely chopped
2 spring onions, finely chopped	2 scallions, finely chopped
½ green pepper, finely chopped	½ green pepper, finely chopped
2 tablespoonsful finely chopped parsley	2½ tablespoonsful finely chopped parsley
1 tablespoonful dried mint	1 tablespoonful dried mint
Paprika	Paprika

1. Mix together the bulgur, rice and salt. Add the water and half the oil and heat thoroughly, then leave to stand for 10 minutes.

2. Heat the remaining oil and add the chopped onions, *sautéing* them until soft.

3. Add the onions and oil to the rice and bulgur mixture.

4. Combine the mixture well, either by hand or in a blender, in which case work with only a small amount at a time, adding water if necessary.

5. When the mixture is smooth and sticky, mix in half the spring onions (scallions), peppers, parsley and mint.

6. Keeping the hands moist, shape into small patties (small torpedo shapes), then deep fry them in vegetable oil until crisp and golden.

7. Serve garnished with the remaining ingredients and a sprinkling of paprika.

Note: These are also delicious served with a yogurt sauce and wedges of lemon.

9.

ORIENTAL RECIPES

Brown rice is the traditional staple diet of the countries of the East and it was not until the advent of colonialism and rice polishing that white rice became a popular food of 'advanced' civilization. Even among the Asian community in Britain consumption of brown rice is practically non-existent and a prejudice against it as the food of peasants will take a long time to disappear.

The pantheons of the early religions of many Eastern countries included a deity whose sole responsibility lay in ensuring a rice harvest of ample quantity and good quality, and perhaps also to ensure successful preparation of some of the recipes listed here.

Preparing Sushi

1

sushi mat

vegetables

rice

nori

2   cut into slices

3   serve cold

SUSHI

For *hors d'oeuvres*, picnics and the lunchbox, sushi is a delightful way to combine brown rice and vegetables with the goodness of seaweed. To be successful with sushi you really need a 'sushi mat', made of strips of bamboo strung together. They are sold in Oriental shops and also appear in many hardware shops being sold as place mats. In fact, if you cannot find a genuine sushi mat, a bamboo place mat will do, although try to find one that has not been dyed. You will need soft rice for sushi, so cook with 2½-3 parts water, depending on whether you use a pressure cooker or not.

Imperial (Metric)
1 sheet nori seaweed*
1½ cupsful soft brown rice
¼ cupful grated carrot
2 tablespoonsful chopped
    watercress

American
1 sheet nori seaweed*
1⅔ cupsful soft brown rice
¼ cupful grated carrot
2½ tablespoonsful chopped
    watercress

1. Toast the nori seaweed by waving it gently above a low flame — the colour will change and it will crisp slightly. Place a sheet of nori on the sushi mat.

2. Lay a thin layer of rice across half the sheet, and lay the vegetables in a row down the centre of the rice.

3. With wet fingers, and using the mat to keep things even and steady, roll the nori sheet over the rice and filling. (This should be one complete turn, using the remainder of the nori to rewrap the rice to make a firm outer skin.)

4. Cut into lengths of 1-1½ inches (25-40mm) long.

Note: You can vary the vegetable part of the filling, and for a long-lasting sushi suitable for camping trips or journeys, put a bit of finely chopped umeboshi plum in the centre — it will stay fresh for days. Other variations for filling include chopped parsley, toasted sunflower seeds and currants, or any finely chopped cooked vegetables.

*Nori seaweed is a variety of laver which has been dried into flat, paper-like sheets.

ADZUKI MOCHI

Imperial (Metric)	American
2 cupsful sweet brown rice (or plain brown rice if sweet is not available)	2½ cupsful sweet brown rice (or plain brown rice if sweet is not available)
½ cupful adzuki beans	½ cupful adzuki beans
4½ cupsful water	5½ cupsful water
½ teaspoonful sea salt	½ teaspoonful sea salt
¼ cupful sesame seeds	¼ cupful sesame seeds
Vegetable oil	Vegetable oil

1. Pressure cook the rice and beans together. (Bring the cooker up to pressure, then lower flame and cook for three minutes.)

2. Leave pan standing undisturbed for a further half an hour.

3. If you do not have a pressure cooker, boil the beans in a pan with lid for 30 minutes in 1½/2 (US) cupsful of water. Add the rice and 3/3½ (US) cupsful more of water and bring back to boil. Cover pan and simmer for 40 minutes. Turn off heat and let stand undisturbed for a further half an hour.

4. Whilst it is still hot, remove about half the mixture and transfer to a food mill. *Purée* the mixture until it becomes very soft, and then add to the remaining rice and bean mixture.

5. Add the salt, then wet your hands and knead the mixture until blended (if it is too sticky, keep wetting hands with cold water).

6. Shape into little cakes approx. half an inch (10-15mm) thick and sprinkle each one with sesame seeds. These can be lightly fried in a heavy frying-pan/skillet brushed with oil or baked for 20 minutes in a moderate oven (turn after ten minutes) or shaped into small balls and deep fried.

Note: Nuts, dried fruits, grated apples etc. can be added to make a sweet dessert mochi either cooked with the rice and beans or added just before cooking. Mochi cakes should be refrigerated if not eaten immediately. Uncooked cakes will keep refrigerated for several days until needed.

RICE WITH ALMONDS AND DATES

Imperial (Metric)	American
1 oz (25g) butter	2½ tablespoonsful butter
½ lb (¼ kilo) long grain brown rice	1 cupful long grain brown rice
1½ cupsful boiling water	1⅔ cupsful boiling water
1 teaspoonful sea salt	1 teaspoonful sea salt

Dressing:

Imperial (Metric)	American
1 oz (25g) butter	2½ tablespoonsful butter
2 oz (50g) blanched almonds	½ cupful blanched almonds
3 oz (75g) dates (stoned)	½ cupful dates (stoned)
2 oz (50g) seedless raisins or sultanas	⅓ cupful seedless raisins or golden seedless raisins
1 teaspoonful rosewater	1 teaspoonful rosewater

1. Melt the butter in a pressure cooker or heavy-bottomed saucepan, whichever you plan to cook the rice in.

2. Add the rice and stir well to coat the grains in the butter.

3. Add the boiling water and salt and boil vigorously for a moment or two, then cover and cook for 40 minutes.

4. Remove from heat, remove lid and cover with a towel. Set aside for 10 minutes.

5. Melt the butter for the dressing in a large frying-pan/skillet, add the almonds and fry gently until they turn golden.

6. Add the dates and raisins or sultanas, fry for 5 minutes and stir constantly.

7. Remove from the heat and stir in the rosewater.

8. Serve with the dressing spooned over the basic rice mixture.

Note: This method of rice preparation is the basic 'pilau' rice recipe which I shall refer to in later recipes.

FESTIVE PILAU

Imperial (Metric)
1 oz (25g) butter
½ lb (¼ kilo) long grain brown rice
1 teaspoonful sea salt
1½ cupsful boiling water

American
2½ tablespoonsful butter
1 cupful long grain brown rice
1 teaspoonful sea salt
1⅔ cupsful boiling water

Sauce:

Imperial (Metric)
1 oz (25g) butter
2 oz (50g) apricots, soaked
2 oz (50g) prunes, soaked
2 oz (50g) sultanas
2 oz (50g) blanched almonds, slivered
1 tablespoonful apple concentrate
1 tablespoonful hot water

American
2½ tablespoonsful butter
⅓ cupful apricots, soaked
⅓ cupful prunes, soaked
⅓ cupful golden seedless raisins
½ cupful blanched almonds, slivered
1 tablespoonful apple concentrate
1 tablespoonful hot water

1. Prepare the rice as in the recipe for Rice with Almonds and Dates (page 94).

2. Melt the butter in a heavy-bottomed saucepan.

3. Add the fruit and almonds and fry together, stirring constantly until the almonds are lightly browned.

4. Mix the apple concentrate together with the water and pour over the fruit in the pan.

5. Cook very gently for about ten minutes, stirring frequently.

6. Serve with the sauce poured over the top of the pilau.

VEGETABLE AND LENTIL PILAU

Imperial (Metric)	American
1 onion, chopped	1 onion, chopped
4 cloves garlic, finely chopped	4 cloves garlic, finely chopped
3 tablespoonsful ghee or vegetable oil	3½ tablespoonsful ghee or vegetable oil
3 cupsful cooked brown rice	3¾ cupsful cooked brown rice
1 teaspoonful coriander	1 teaspoonful cilantro
1 teaspoonful sea salt	1 teaspoonful sea salt
6 cloves	6 cloves
1 teaspoonful cinnamon	1 teaspoonful cinnamon
1 teaspoonful ginger	1 teaspoonful ginger
1 teaspoonful freshly ground black pepper	1 teaspoonful freshly ground black pepper
2 bay leaves	2 bay leaves
1 lb (½ kilo) mixed vegetables, chopped	1 pound mixed vegetables, chopped
3 tomatoes, quartered	3 tomatoes, quartered
2 cupsful lentils, cooked and drained	2½ cupsful lentils, cooked and drained
4 oz (100g) spinach or greens, chopped	4 ounces spinach or greens, chopped

1. Fry the onion and garlic in 1 tablespoonful of ghee until golden.

2. Add the rice and spices and stir-fry for 5 minutes.

3. *Sauté* the chopped vegetables and tomatoes separately in 1 tablespoonful of ghee until tender.

4. Fry the drained lentils with the chopped spinach in 1 tablespoonful of ghee for a few minutes.

5. Add all the pre-cooked vegetables to the rice and onion mixture and stir gently for 5 minutes.

6. Serve garnished with chopped coriander (cilantro) or parsley.

YELLOW RICE PILAU

Imperial (Metric)	American
2 onions, sliced	2 onions, sliced
2 tablespoonsful ghee or vegetable oil	2½ tablespoonsful ghee or vegetable oil
3 cupsful long grain brown rice, cooked	3¾ cupsful long grain brown rice, cooked
½ teaspoonful curry powder	½ teaspoonful curry powder
10 peppercorns	10 perppercorns
4 cloves	4 cloves
1 teaspoonful turmeric	1 teaspoonful turmeric
1½ cupsful unsweetened grated coconut	1⅔ cupsful unsweetened grated coconut
1 teaspoonful sea salt	1 teaspoonful sea salt
10 almonds, blanched and chopped	10 almonds, blanched and chopped
10 cashew nuts, chopped	10 cashew nuts, chopped

1. Fry the onions in 1½ tablespoonsful of ghee until golden. (Keep a little onion aside for garnishing.)

2. Add the rice, spices, coconut and salt, and stir-fry gently until the rice becomes yellow.

3. Fry the nuts and remaining onion in the ghee and use to garnish.

CAULIFLOWER PILAU

Imperial (Metric)
½ lb (¼ kilo) cauliflower sprigs
2 teaspoonsful sea salt
Freshly ground black pepper
2 tablespoonsful ghee or vegetable
  oil
1 onion, chopped
6 cloves garlic, finely chopped
½ teaspoonful cinnamon
6 cloves
1 teaspoonful ginger
½ teaspoonful paprika
1 teaspoonful cumin
½ teaspoonful garam masala
3 cupsful cooked brown rice
1 cupful plain yogurt

American
8 ounces cauliflower sprigs
2 teaspoonsful sea salt
Freshly ground black pepper
2½ tablespoonsful ghee or vegetable
  oil
1 onion, chopped
6 cloves garlic, finely chopped
½ teaspoonful cinnamon
6 cloves
1 teaspoonful ginger
½ teaspoonful paprika
1 teaspoonful cumin
½ teaspoonful garam masala
3¾ cupsful cooked brown rice
1¼ cupsful plain yogurt

1. Sprinkle the cauliflower sprigs with salt and pepper and fry in ghee until they begin to turn golden.

2. Remove from the pan and fry the onion and garlic. Replace the cauliflower and add the spices and rice and stir-fry for 5 minutes.

3. Stir in the yogurt and cook for another few minutes. Garnish with finely sliced onion and tomatoes.

PEAS PILAU

Imperial (Metric)	American
1 onion, chopped	1 onion, chopped
4 cloves garlic, finely chopped	4 cloves garlic, finely chopped
2 tablespoonsful ghee or vegetable oil	2½ tablespoonsful ghee or vegetable oil
3 cupsful long grain brown rice, cooked	3¾ cupsful long grain brown rice, cooked
¼ teaspoonful ginger	¼ teaspoonful ginger
6 cloves	6 cloves
1 teaspoonful cinnamon	1 teaspoonful cinnamon
½ teaspoonful paprika	½ teaspoonful paprika
1 teaspoonful garam masala	1 teaspoonful garam masala
1 teaspoonful cumin	1 teaspoonful cumin
1 teaspoonful sea salt	1 teaspoonful sea salt
1½ cupsful fresh or frozen peas	1⅔ cupsful fresh or frozen peas

1. Fry the onion and garlic in ghee until golden.

2. Add the remaining ingredients and stir-fry until the peas are cooked.

3. Serve with vegetable curry and yogurt.

PILAU RICE

Imperial (Metric)	American
1 onion, sliced	1 onion, sliced
4 cloves garlic, finely chopped	4 cloves garlic, finely chopped
1 tablespoonful ghee or vegetable oil	1 tablespoonful ghee or vegetable oil
3 cupsful long grain brown rice, pre-cooked but still firm	3¾ cupsful long grain brown rice, pre-cooked but still firm
1 piece of ginger, finely chopped	1 piece of ginger, finely chopped
6 cloves	6 cloves
A few pieces of broken cinnamon	A few pieces of broken cinnamon
½ teaspoonful paprika	½ teaspoonful paprika
1 teaspoonful garam masala	1 teaspoonful garam masala
1 teaspoonful cumin	1 teaspoonful cumin
½ teaspoonful sea salt	½ teaspoonful sea salt
½ cupful water or vegetable stock, boiling	½ cupful water or vegetable stock, boiling
Fresh coriander or parsley to garnish, chopped	Fresh cilantro or parsley to garnish, chopped

1. *Sauté* the garlic and half the onion in a heavy frying-pan (skillet) until golden.

2. Add the rice, spices and seasoning and stir-fry until the rice grains become lightly coloured.

3. Add the water or stock, cover the pan and simmer gently until the liquid is absorbed.

4. Serve garnished with the remaining onion (fried) and coriander (cilantro) or parsley.

BEETROOT RICE

Imperial (Metric)	American
2 onions, chopped	2 onions, chopped
2 tablespoonsful ghee or vegetable oil	2½ tablespoonsful ghee or vegetable oil
1 teaspoonful mustard seeds	1 teaspoonful mustard seeds
1 teaspoonful freshly ground black pepper	1 teaspoonful freshly ground black pepper
½ teaspoonful cumin	½ teaspoonful cumin
½ teaspoonful turmeric	½ teaspoonful turmeric
1 large beetroot, cooked and diced	1 large beet, cooked and diced
½ teaspoonful sea salt	½ teaspoonful sea salt
3 cupsful brown rice, cooked	3¾ cupsful brown rice, cooked
Juice of 1 lemon	Juice of 1 lemon
10 cashew nuts, chopped	10 cashew nuts, chopped

1. Fry the onions in the ghee. Add the spices and cook gently for a few minutes.

2. Add the beetroot (beet) and salt and mix well with the rice.

3. Sprinkle with lemon juice, garnish with fried cashew nuts and serve hot with yogurt.

INDIAN SAVOURY RICE

Imperial (Metric)
2 tablespoonsful ghee or vegetable oil
3 cupsful cooked long grain brown rice
1 teaspoonful cumin

American
2½ tablespoonsful ghee or vegetable oil
3¾ cupsful cooked long grain brown rice
1 teaspoonful cumin

1. Heat ghee in heavy skillet.

2. Stir in rice and cumin, mix well and serve hot.

SPICY RICE

Imperial (Metric)
1 onion, finely chopped
½ cupful chopped cashew nuts
½ cupful sultanas
¼ cupful grated unsweetened coconut
2 tablespoonsful ghee or vegetable oil
3 cupsful cooked long grain brown rice
¾ teaspoonful fennel seeds
½ teaspoonful cumin
½ teaspoonful fenugreek
½ teaspoonful poppy seeds
½ teaspoonful mustard seeds
1 teaspoonful turmeric

American
1 onion, finely chopped
½ cupful chopped cashew nuts
½ cupful golden seedless raisins
¼ cupful grated unsweetened coconut
2½ tablespoonsful ghee or vegetable oil
3¾ cupsful cooked long grain brown rice
¾ teaspoonful fennel seeds
½ teaspoonful cumin
½ teaspoonful fenugreek
½ teaspoonful poppy seeds
½ teaspoonful mustard seeds
1 teaspoonful turmeric

1. *Sauté* the onion, nuts, sultanas (golden seedless raisins) and coconut in a tablespoonful of ghee.

2. Stir in the cooked rice, then fry all the spices in the remaining ghee and mix them into the rice until the grains become yellow.

Note: Sesame and caraway seeds can be used for variation.

COCONUT RICE

Imperial (Metric)	American
1 tablespoonful ghee	1 tablespoonful ghee
1 large onion, finely chopped	1 large onion, finely chopped
1/2 teaspoonful turmeric	1/2 teaspoonful turmeric
1 teaspoonful sea salt	1 teaspoonful sea salt
6 cloves	6 cloves
10 peppercorns	10 peppercorns
3 cupsful long grain brown rice, pre-cooked but firm	3¾ cupsful long grain brown rice, pre-cooked but firm
1½ cupsful desiccated unsweetened coconut	1⅔ cupsful desiccated unsweetened coconut

1. Melt ghee in heavy frying-pan (skillet) and *sauté* onion lightly until transparent.

2. Stir in the turmeric, salt, cloves and peppercorns.

3. Add rice and coconut and fry gently together, stirring constantly, for 10 minutes.

MUSHROOM PILAU

Imperial (Metric)	American
1 onion, sliced	1 onion, sliced
1 tablespoonful ghee	1 tablespoonful ghee
2 cupsful long grain brown rice, cooked	2½ cupsful long grain brown rice, cooked
1 cupful mushrooms	1¼ cupsful mushrooms
½ teaspoonful sea salt	½ teaspoonful sea salt
½ cupful peas	½ cupful peas
½ cupful water or vegetable stock, boiling	½ cupful water or vegetable stock, boiling

1. *Sauté* the onion in ghee until golden.

2. Stir in the rice, mushrooms, salt, peas and add the water or stock.

3. Cover and simmer gently for 10 minutes.

10.
RICE AND TOMATO DISHES

Brown rice and cooked tomatoes provide a very satisfying harmony of flavours, sweet, piquant, and savoury all at once. Italian and Spanish cuisine in particular owe a great deal to this marriage of flavours.

In the nineteenth century a Colonel Johnson broke a longstanding prejudice against tomatoes by eating one on the steps of the courthouse of his home town in Massachusetts. Doctors were in attendance and several people sought to have him restrained as tomatoes were widely believed to be poisonous and were grown for their decorative value only. In fact tomatoes *are*, like potatoes and aubergines (eggplants), a member of the nightshade family, which also includes belladonna and *Datura stramonium*. The active ingredient of these plants, atropine, can cause delirium but usually just leads to disturbed sleep and dreams. An article in the December 1978 edition of *Scientific American* describes research to breed hybrid tomatoes that are completely free of these alkaloids so they can be enjoyed in limitless quantities by all, even those who are particularly sensitive to vegetables from the nightshade family.

STUFFED TOMATOES 1

Imperial (Metric)	American
8 well shaped, firm tomatoes	8 well shaped, firm tomatoes
½ cupful chopped mixed nuts	½ cupful chopped mixed nuts
1 chopped onion	1 chopped onion
2 tablespoonsful cooked brown rice	2½ tablespoonsful cooked brown rice
½ tablespoonful chopped mint	½ tablespoonful chopped mint
Pinch of dill	Pinch of dill
Pinch each of sea salt and freshly ground black pepper	Pinch each of sea salt and freshly ground black pepper
2 tablespoonsful vegetable oil	2½ tablespoonsful vegetable oil
3 tablespoonsful butter or polyunsaturated margarine	3½ tablespoonsful butter or polyunsaturated margarine
½ cupful vegetable stock or water	½ cupful vegetable stock or water

1. Several hours before required, slice tops off tomatoes and set these to one side.

2. Carefully remove pith and seeds and discard.

3. *Sauté* the remaining ingredients in oil, then gently fill the tomatoes and replace the lids.

4. Place tomatoes in an oiled casserole dish, put a dab of butter on each tomato and pour in the stock.

5. Cover the dish and bake in pre-heated oven at 375°F/190°C (Gas Mark 5) until tomatoes are cooked — about 30 minutes.

STUFFED TOMATOES 2

Imperial (Metric)
6 firm tomatoes
1 large onion, chopped
1 large stick celery, finely chopped
½ cupful mushrooms, chopped
2 tablespoonsful olive oil
½ cupful cooked brown rice
½ cupful wholemeal breadcrumbs
Thyme
Real soya sauce

American
6 firm tomatoes
1 large onion, chopped
1 large stick celery, finely chopped
½ cupful mushrooms, chopped
2½ tablespoonsful olive oil
½ cupful cooked brown rice
½ cupful wholemeal breadcrumbs
Thyme
Real soya sauce

1. Stand tomatoes on stalk ends and slice off tops at the more pointed end.

2. Scoop out seeds and core with a knife and teaspoon.

3. *Sauté* onion, celery and mushrooms in oil until onion is soft and translucent, then add rice, breadcrumbs, thyme and season with soya sauce. (The mixture should be moist.)

4. Fill the hollowed out tomatoes, replace the tops, brush with oil and bake in a hot oven at 425°F/220°C (Gas Mark 7) for 15-20 minutes.

MUSHROOM AND TOMATO RISOTTO

Imperial (Metric)	American
1 large onion, chopped	1 large onion, chopped
4 tablespoonsful olive oil	5 tablespoonsful olive oil
½ lb (¼ kilo) small mushrooms, sliced	4 cupsful small mushrooms, sliced
2 cupsful long grain brown rice	2½ cupsful long grain brown rice
4 cupsful boiling water	5 cupsful boiling water
2 cloves garlic, crushed	2 cloves garlic, crushed
1 lb (½ kilo) tomatoes, peeled, seeded and chopped	1 pound tomatoes, peeled, seeded and chopped
1 tablespoonful real soya sauce	1 tablespoonful real soya sauce
1 teaspoonful thyme	1 teaspoonful thyme
1 teaspoonful oregano or marjoram	1 teaspoonful oregano or marjoram

1. *Sauté* half the onion in half the oil, add the mushrooms and *sauté* for another 4 minutes.

2. Add the rice and stir-fry for another 2 or 3 minutes. Then add the boiling water and simmer for 40-45 minutes.

3. In another pan *sauté* the remaining onion, adding the garlic after a few minutes. Add the tomatoes and simmer gently until the sauce thickens, about 20 minutes, adding a little water and the soya sauce.

4. Add the herbs a few minutes before removing the sauce from the heat, then combine the sauce with the rice.

5. Cover for 10 minutes to allow the flavours to combine, then serve.

11.

DAIRY FOODS

Dairy products combine well with rice, and the bran content of brown rice helps to counteract the digestive sluggishness many people associate with cheesy and milky foods. Yogurt in particular can be added to many of the recipes in other sections of this book, especially rice and cauliflower (see page 40).

RICE AND ALMOND CASSEROLE

Imperial (Metric)
2 cupsful cooked brown rice
2 beaten eggs
2 cupsful milk
2 tablespoonsful vegetable oil
1 tablespoonful real soya sauce
1 cupful chopped lightly toasted almonds (cashew pieces or chopped toasted hazels can be used instead)

American
2½ cupsful cooked brown rice
2 beaten eggs
2½ cupsful milk
2½ tablespoonsful vegetable oil
1 tablespoonful real soya sauce
1¼ cupsful chopped lightly toasted almonds (cashew pieces or chopped toasted hazels can be used instead)

1. Combine ingredients and pour into an oiled casserole of at least 2 pints/1 litre capacity.

2. Bake at 350°F/180°C (Gas Mark 4) until the mixture has set and formed a light brown skin — about 25-30 minutes.

YOGURT SAUCE

Imperial (Metric)
1 cupful goat's milk yogurt
½ cupful chopped chives (other
    herbs such as parsley, chervil or
    fresh basil can be used in place or
    as well as chives)
1 or 2 cloves garlic, crushed

American
1¼ cupful goat's milk yogurt
½ cupful chopped chives (other
    herbs such as parsley, chervil or
    fresh basil can be used in place or
    as well as chives)
1 or 2 cloves garlic, crushed

Mix all ingredients together and serve over hot rice.

RIZ GRUYÈRE

For this recipe you can use Gruyère or Emmenthal cheese for that authentic *fondue* flavour, although if you can get a Fribourg or Tomme de Savoir, use it by all means.

Imperial (Metric)	American
2 cupsful sliced onions	2½ cupsful sliced onions
3 celery stalks, chopped	3 celery stalks, chopped
2 carrots, diced	2 carrots, diced
4 oz (100g) mushrooms, sliced	2 cupsful mushrooms, sliced
Vegetable oil	Vegetable oil
½ cupful chopped parsley	½ cupful chopped parsley
2 cloves finely chopped garlic	2 cloves finely chopped garlic
1 teaspoonful paprika powder	1 teaspoonful paprika powder
¼ teaspoonful ground ginger	¼ teaspoonful ground ginger
2 teaspoonsful real soya sauce	2 teaspoonsful real soya sauce
3 cupsful cooked brown rice	3¾ cupsful cooked brown rice
1 lb (½ kilo) grated cheese	4 cupsful grated cheese

1. *Sauté* the vegetables in oil until the onions are soft.

2. Add the parsley, garlic, spices and soya sauce.

3. In a shallow casserole, place thin alternate layers of brown rice, cooked vegetable mixture and grated cheese.

4. Top with grated cheese and bake for half an hour at 350°F/180°C (Gas Mark 4).

STILTON SALAD

While Stilton features in the title of this recipe, Roquefort, blue Wensleydale or even a blue Danish cheese can be used. If you pressure cook the rice, use less water.

Imperial (Metric)	American
1 large onion, coarsely chopped	1 large onion, coarsely chopped
1 clove garlic, chopped	1 clove garlic, chopped
3 tablespoonsful olive oil	3 tablespoonsful olive oil
1 cupful long grain brown rice	1¼ cupsful long grain brown rice
2 cupsful boiling water	2½ cupsful boiling water
1 sweet apple	1 sweet apple
3-4 cupsful crumbled Stilton	3¾-5 cupsful crumbled Stilton

Dressing:

Imperial (Metric)	American
3 tablespoonsful vegetable oil	3½ tablespoonsful vegetable oil
1 tablespoonful lemon juice or cider vinegar	1 tablespoonful lemon juice or cider vinegar
1 clove garlic, crushed	1 clove garlic, crushed

1. *Sauté* the onion and clove of garlic in oil until soft and translucent.

2. Stir in the rice and fry for a couple of minutes.

3. Combine with water and simmer for 30-35 minutes or until water is absorbed.

4. Mix with dressing and leave to cool.

5. When the mixture is cold, core and dice the apple and mix apple and cheese with the rice. Refrigerate before serving.

BAKED EGGS ON A RICE BED

Imperial (Metric)	American
1 onion, chopped	1 onion, chopped
Vegetable oil	Vegetable oil
1 cupful long grain brown rice	1½ cupsful long grain brown rice
Sea salt	Sea salt
Real soya sauce	Real soya sauce
6 eggs	6 eggs
Freshly ground black pepper	Freshly ground black pepper
6 oz (150g) grated sharp cheese (e.g. mature Cheddar)	1½ cupsful grated sharp cheese (e.g. mature Cheddar)
2 tablespoonsful wholewheat breadcrumbs	2½ tablespoonsful wholewheat breadcrumbs

1. *Sauté* onion in oil until soft, then add rice and stir-fry for another three minutes.

2. Cover with 2/2½ (US) cupsful of boiling water and salt or soya sauce to taste and simmer until the water is absorbed (35-40 minutes).

3. Oil a casserole dish and fill with cooked rice mixture.

4. Break the eggs over the bed of rice — the yolks will probably break but this is not important.

5. Sprinkle with the salt and pepper, then sprinkle with the grated cheese and finally add a thin layer of breadcrumbs.

6. Bake for 20-25 minutes at 250°F/130°C (Gas Mark ½). Serve immediately sprinkled with chopped parsley.

RICE SALAD WITH MAYONNAISE

Imperial (Metric)
2 cupsful cooked brown rice
1 cupful peas, cooked
½ cupful celery, finely sliced
½ cupful chopped spring onions
½ cupful chopped tomato
½ cupful mayonnaise
½ cupful sour cream
½ cupful sunflower seeds
Sea salt and freshly ground black
  pepper

American
2½ cupsful cooked brown rice
1¼ cupsful peas, cooked
½ cupful celery, finely sliced
½ cupful chopped scallions
½ cupful chopped tomato
½ cupful mayonnaise
½ cupful sour cream
½ cupful sunflower seeds
Sea salt and freshly ground black
  pepper

1. Combine rice, peas, celery, onions and tomato.

2. Blend the remaining ingredients and stir the mixture into the rice and vegetables. Chill lightly before serving.

12.

SWEETS AND PUDDINGS

Apart from the variations on the theme of rice pudding, brown rice, and the special variety known as sweet brown rice which is grown in Japan and California, forms the base of several other sweet dishes. None of these recipes contain sugar or honey as these sweeteners are only really necessary when the palate has already been jaded by over-use of them.

The natural sweetness of dried fruits, and the rapid effect of saliva enzymes in turning the carbohydrates of rice into dextrins and other natural sugars, produces satisfying sweetness and a marriage of flavours which are not overwhelmed by the dominating sweetness that even a small quantity of sugar introduces.

The advantages of eating a diet that is free of sugar are well known and can be briefly summarized as: less likelihood of indigestion; more true energy; healthy teeth; good bone development in children; sweet breath; a healthy appetite for food and enjoyment of its flavours; and a greatly reduced likelihood of falling victim to several degenerative diseases, including diabetes, heart disease and liver problems.

Eating sugar effects metabolic changes in the body that lead to a reduction in the body's reserves of B vitamins and minerals and stimulate an artificial sense of appetitie for food to replace these losses. It is this excess appetite that contributes at least as much to obesity as the actual carbohydrates consumed in the sugar itself.

There are several natural sweeteners available which do not disrupt the body's natural balance as dramatically as sugar. Maltose, derived from the malting of grains, usually barley, is a good one, especially used in conjunction with grains. Fruit juice concentrates such as apple juice syrup or boiled raisin juice also enhance desserts and natural sweetness.

CHILLED RICE PUDDING

Imperial (Metric)	American
1½ cupsful water	1⅔ cupsful water
1½ cupsful milk	1⅔ cupsful milk
1 cupful plain brown rice	1¼ cupsful plain brown rice
1 cupful sweet brown rice	1¼ cupsful sweet brown rice
¼ cupful ground almonds	¼ cupful ground almonds
2 tablespoonsful apple concentrate	2½ tablespoonsful apple concentrate
Skinned and roasted whole almonds	Skinned and roasted whole almonds

1. Mix water and milk and bring to the boil.

2. Mix the plain and sweet rice, then stir it into the liquid and cover.

3. Cook briskly for 12 minutes.

4. Meanwhile mix almonds and apple concentrate and add to the cooking rice.

5. Turn heat low and simmer for a further 30 minutes.

6. Place in individual dessert dishes and leave to cool. Decorate with whole almonds and chill before serving.

PEACH RICE

Imperial (Metric)
1 cupful grated unsweetened
  coconut
1 lb (½ kilo) peaches, stoned and
  sliced
1 tablespoonful ghee or butter
10 cashew nuts, chopped
1 tablespoonful sultanas
3 cupful cooked brown rice

American
1¼ cupsful grated unsweetened
  coconut
1 pound peaches, stoned and
  sliced
1 tablespoonful ghee or butter
10 cashew nuts, chopped
1 tablespoonful golden seedless
  raisins
3¾ cupsful cooked brown rice

1. Fry the coconut and peaches in the ghee for 5 minutes.

2. Add the cashew nuts and sultanas and cook for a few more minutes.

3. Mix in the rice and stir-fry until hot.

BROWN RICE AND YOGURT SUPREME

Imperial (Metric)
1½ cupsful cooked brown rice
½ lb (¼ kilo) plain yogurt
1 cupful crushed pineapple (well
    drained)
2 bananas, diced

American
1⅔ cupsful cooked brown rice
1 cupful plain yogurt
1¼ cupsful crushed pineapple (well
    drained)
2 bananas, diced

Combine all the ingredients. Chill well before serving.

RICE AND CARROT PUDDING

If you wish, substitute an equal weight of cooked pumpkin for the carrots.

Imperial (Metric)	American
2 cupsful cooked carrots	2½ cupsful cooked carrots
1 cupful cooked short grain brown rice	1¼ cupsful cooked short grain brown rice
¼ cupful fresh apple juice	¼ cupful fresh apple juice
1 tablespoonful apple juice concentrate, barley malt syrup or rice syrup	1 tablespoonful apple juice concentrate, barley malt syrup or rice syrup
2 tablespoonsful hot vegetable oil	2½ tablespoonsful hot vegetable oil
Pinch of each of nutmeg, cinnamon and grated ginger	Pinch each of nutmeg, cinnamon and grated ginger
1 beaten egg	1 beaten egg
½ cupful currants or raisins	½ cupful currants or raisins

1. *Purée* carrots and add all ingredients. Mix thoroughly, adding more apple juice if needed.

2. Bake in an oiled baking dish at 350°F/180°C (Gas Mark 4) for 30-40 minutes. (Place the baking dish in a larger pan with one-inch (25mm) depth of water to prevent scorching when in the oven.)

BROWN RICE AND APRICOT LAYER PUDDING

Imperial (Metric)
2 cupsful dried apricots (soaked for at least 3 hours beforehand)
4 cupsful cooked brown rice
1 teaspoonful apple concentrate
½ pint (¼ litre) milk
1 teaspoonful cinnamon
½ cupful roasted almonds, slivered

American
2½ cupsful dried apricots (soaked for at least 3 hours beforehand)
5 cupsful cooked brown rice
1 teaspoonful apple concentrate
1⅓ cupsful milk
1 teaspoonful cinnamon
½ cupful roasted almonds, slivered

1. Lay half of the apricots on the bottom of a casserole dish.

2. Spread half the rice on the top, then lay the remaining apricots on top and cover this layer with the rest of the rice.

3. Stir the apple concentrate into the milk with the cinnamon and pour the heated milk mixture over the rice and apricots.

4. Bake at 350°F/180°C (Gas Mark 4) for about 30 minutes, then serve with slivered and roasted almonds on top.

RICE PUDDING

Imperial (Metric)	American
4 cupsful cooked sweet brown rice	5 cupsful cooked sweet brown rice
1 cupful raisins	1¼ cupsful raisins
2 cupsful milk	2½ cupsful milk
1 teaspoonful mixed spice	1 teaspoonful mixed spice
1 teaspoonful nutmeg	1 teaspoonful nutmeg
1 cupful desiccated unsweetened coconut	1¼ cupsful desiccated unsweetened coconut

Mix all ingredients together and bake in a deep dish at 450°F/230°C (Gas Mark 8).

13.

BROWN RICE AND FASTING

One of the greatest factors that has led to the widespread consumption of brown rice is the spread of the macrobiotic way of eating in the United States and Europe in the past decade. The macrobiotic philosophy, based on the dialectical principle of Yin and Yang, enables a person to judge the correct balance of his eating without recourse to calorie charts or lists of mineral and vitamin contents of food.

The macrobiotic diet is primarily a preventive and positive diet, seeking to maximize the mental and spiritual potential of the individual through maintaining a body that, through good diet and regular activity, is functioning at the peak of its capabilities. However, few people can carry through the transition from a conventional diet based on processed refined foods, with sugar and chemical additives, without being drawn back to eating habits that not only undermine the body's efficiency but also lead to ill health.

As a means of enabling the body to repair itself Georges Ohsawa, the founder of modern macrobiotic philosophy, introduced Diet Number Seven, a diet based solely on brown rice which enabled the body's natural cleansing functions to work free of any input of rich and unbalancing foods whilst still maintaining a fundamental level of balanced nutrition. Much disease originates in intestinal malfunction which results in poor blood quality, and, by restoring intestinal motility and effectiveness, the brown rice diet can lead to a cure of many chronic conditions.

Many people have experienced fasting over a period of a week or more and have realized that after an initial difficult period, going without food is not a very distressing process. With practice, fasting becomes much easier and fast days and other variations on fasting themes are a traditional feature of all the world's religions.

A fast using brown rice is an easy way of enjoying all of fasting's benefits without having to do without food entirely. It also cultivates an awareness and appreciation of the advantages of careful chewing, enhances one's enjoyment of the flavour of brown rice, and leads to a greater understanding of the role of rice and other whole cereals as the fulcrum in balancing one's nutrition.

It is not advisable to eat a diet based exlusively on brown rice for more than a few days at the outset, and one should not exceed a week on the diet without good reason, preferably with medical consultation. Case histories are available of individuals who have obtained remission of cancer and other diseases using a brown rice based regimen in a booklet called *A Dietary Approach to Cancer* (available from East-West Centre, 188 Old Street, London EC1).

A brown rice fast can include small amounts of the following foods: sea salt used in preparation of the rice; *gomasio* sesame salt; *tamari* soya sauce; and *tahini* sesame seed cream. *Gomasio* is made by combining eight parts of lightly toasted sesame seeds with one part of sea salt and grinding them together either in a pestle and mortar or a pepper mill. Ready-made *gomasios* are available from many natural food shops, but they lack the flavour of the freshly made condiment. Drinks should be limited to mineral water and herbal teas.

A rice gruel can be made by adding water to cooked rice to the desired consistency and this, lightly seasoned with soya sauce or *gomasio*, is an ideal way of getting invalids to take food, as well as being a variation to include in a brown rice fast.

Always remember, unless you are used to fasting, the effects not only on your metabolism but also your psyche can be unbalancing at first and care should be taken not to overtax yourself or to engage in activities that call for full concentration such as operating machinery or driving a car.

Preparing Brown Rice for Fasting

Sesame Rice. Lightly toast whole sesame seeds in an unoiled frying pan. Stir into the rice, about one tablespoonful of seeds per cupful of cooked rice.

Umeboshi Rice. De-stone a few umeboshi plums and break up the flesh of the plum into four or five pieces and scatter over the rice before cooking. (Use no salt in preparing the rice as there is an adequate amount in the plum.)

Miso Rice. Dissolve a teaspoonful of *miso* soyabean paste in each cupful of water used in preparing the rice. Boil the rice in the usual way. If you are pressure cooking the rice use one third less *miso* per cupful of water. *Miso, tamari,* or *shoyu* soya sauce can also be added after cooking the rice, but the flavour infuses the grains if added before cooking. In using these remember not to add any salt before cooking.

Herb Rice. You may wish to include a specific herb in your diet such as parsley, mugwort, thyme, etc. When the rice is cooked, stir in a teaspoonful or so of the herb and allow to stand for another ten minutes. The steam and heat of the rice will draw out the herbal flavours. Adding herbs before cooking will lead to overcooking the herbs and either losing their flavour or, in some cases, drawing out a bitter element that is not desirable.

Raw Rice. For intestinal problems, and particularly for purging intestinal parasites, a handful of raw rice eaten as the first food of the day, and chewed very thoroughly, can be very effective. Raw food is always beneficial to the digestive system as it is assimilated farther down the intestines than cooked food, and raw grains in small quantities can be very effective in restoring tone and vitality to this important organ.

Raw rice can also be lightly roasted until slightly browned in colour for a nuttier flavour.

INDEX